REMEMBERING

katharine hepburn

REMEMBERING

katharine hepburn

Stories of Wit and Wisdom
About America's Leading Lady

ANN NYBERG

Globe
Pequot

Guilford, Connecticut

Globe
Pequot

An imprint of Rowman & Littlefield

Distributed by NATIONAL BOOK NETWORK

British Library Cataloguing in Publication Information Available
Library of Congress Cataloging-in-Publication Data available

ISBN 978-1-4930-2545-9
ISBN (e-book) 978-1-4930-2546-6

The paper used in this publication meets the minimum requirements of American National Standard for Information Sciences—Permanence of Paper for Printed Library Materials, ANSI/NISO Z39.48-1992.

Interior design by Jen Huppert Design

Kate in the 1940s

for kate

contents

acknowledgments

The vignettes in this book are a true gift for anyone who wants a glimpse inside the real life of Katharine Hepburn—Connecticut gal who rose to the stars. I wish to thank the many people who took the time to be interviewed by me and share their stories—this book would not exist without them.

I especially want to thank the late Ellsworth Grant, Katharine's brother-in-law, who was an observer of much of her life. A few years before his death, Ellsworth graciously shared a number of stories with me (he even gave me a typed copy of them and said, "This is for you."—probably to be sure I got them correct). As a journalist I am so happy to share these with so many others. As I retyped his vignettes for portions of this book, I felt his heart and soul in the writing and I decided

these were best retold in his own words. A tremendous thank you to Ellsworth.

The author with Ellsworth Grant.

Circa 1943

introduction

Born on Hudson Street in Hartford, Connecticut, on May 12, 1907, to Katharine Martha Houghton and Dr. Thomas Norval Hepburn, Katharine Houghton Hepburn would become a legend. She grew up one of six children in a lovely Victorian home at the end of Forest Street. This area, best known as Nook Farm, was home to a coterie of literary activists, including Mark Twain, Harriet Beecher Stowe, and Isabella Beecher Hooker.

Hepburn's movie gowns on display.

Hepburn was brash, outspoken, ambitious, a control freak, unpredictable, and on record as saying, "I have an everlasting ego." She was also a New England beauty. She wore trousers when most women in the 1920s and '30s were wearing dresses. She did not follow the leader, ever, and in so doing, made herself an icon.

Hepburn set her course early. During the time she was a student at Bryn Mawr College in Pennsylvania, she announced to her family that she would become an actress. She graduated with a degree in history in 1926, and took charge from the get go. She married Ludlow "Luddy" Ogden Smith in 1928, but divorced him a mere six years later amid fears he would stand in the way of her success. They did, however, remain close friends until the end of their lives.

Katharine as a child.

It is written that Luddy financed the stage play of *The Philadelphia Story* in 1939 that helped restart Hepburn's then fledgling career. That play, which then lead to the blockbuster movie by the same name, put her back in the star column forever more.

Hepburn earned her first Oscar in 1934 for a film called *Morning Glory,* but faltered after that. She would star in a play on Broadway called *The Lake,* which was a disaster. In 1937 she made a movie with RKO Studios called *Stage Door* alongside actress-dancer Ginger Rogers. That, too, was a flop. Then there was *Bringing Up Baby* in which Hepburn starred with Cary Grant in 1938. It went flat. After that, she was labeled box office poison and left RKO.

It was around this time that a very wealthy, good-looking, business tycoon and aviator named Howard Hughes came into Hepburn's life, and things started to ignite—personally and professionally. For a time the two were "all in." While they were dating, Hughes landed his water plane at her Fenwick home. A marriage never materialized, but he is credited with also helping to turn around her career and catapult her once again into stardom.

While there was glory again career-wise in 1938, there was also enormous tragedy. A deadly and disastrous hurricane roared up the coast of New England, killing nearly 700 people and damaging or destroying an estimated 57,000 homes. Hepburn's shingle-style Fenwick family estate was one of them. Nothing was left except a few trinkets found here and there. Almost immediately she started rebuilding, this time using brick. As the story goes it was finished for

Morning Glory (1933) with Adolphe Menjou (left) and Douglas Fairbanks, Jr.

the summer season the next year so that the Hepburns would not miss out on the "season" in Fenwick.

Katharine Hepburn had good instincts when it came to show business. When *The Philadelphia Story* was written loosely based on her life, she bought the rights to the story. She had a hunch that everyone would want a piece of it and took it to Hollywood. MGM produced it in 1940; George Cukor directed it. Hepburn starred opposite two leading men in Hollywood—Henry Fonda and Cary Grant. Her hunch was right, it was a huge hit landing six Oscar nominations.

Likewise, Hepburn continued to build on her career. In 1941 a movie called *Woman of The Year* came along in which Hepburn co-starred with Spencer Tracy, a married man who would become the love of her life. The pair was box office magic. They were together personally and professionally until his death in 1967. Their last movie together was *Guess Who's Coming To Dinner*. By then Tracy was very ill from years of abusing alcohol, but Hepburn bolstered him through the film. He died three weeks after it wrapped. Hepburn won her second Oscar for the film.

Her third Oscar was for the film *Lion In The Winter* starring opposite Peter O'Toole. As Director Anthony Harvey tells it, the two did not get along, but on-screen no one knew. Hepburn was an actress through and through.

In 1982 Hepburn co-starred with Henry Fonda in *On Golden Pond*. They both won oscars for their performances.

The Iconic Katharine Hepburn

Whether it concerned her movies, her life, her politics, her sense of style, or her love for Spencer Tracy, Hepburn was a woman way ahead of her time. Her spunk continues to be admired by many. She moved through life by taking control, always. It seems every facet of her life was fascinating; she even called herself "fascinating." To this day, years after her death, people still want to know what made her tick.

At the time Hepburn was in Hollywood, she defied most norms. She set herself apart from other actresses from a very young age. She was indeed bold, brash, and beautiful.

Circa 1940

Even though Hepburn received four leading actress Academy Awards during her decades-long acting career, the most any woman has ever won, she never showed up to accept them. She went on record as saying she was afraid she wouldn't win. The only time Hepburn showed up at the annual ceremony was in 1974 for the forty-sixth Annual Academy Awards. She was there to present the Irving G. Thalberg Memorial Award to producer Lawrence Weingarten. She walked on stage, after being introduced by actor David Niven, wearing pants—a bold move for a woman in that time. All of her acting peers in the room stood and gave her a thunderous round of applause. Watching the video of this rare moment, you can see the pure joy on Hepburn's face. It's as if she had waited her entire life for such acceptance. Hepburn took it all in. Then she started to speak.

> "ACTING IS THE PERFECT IDIOT'S PROFESSION." —*katharine hepburn*

"Thank you, very, very much. I am naturally deeply moved, I'm also very happy that I didn't hear anyone call out . . . it's about time." And then she made this admission, "I'm living proof that a person can wait forty-one years to be unselfish."

To those words there was more applause. Her only moment on stage at the Academy Awards came forty-one years after she won her

You'll note that her first Oscar is much smaller than the other three. Won in 1934 for *Morning Glory*, it is gold-plated and solid bronze.

first Oscar. Hepburn's Oscars on display at the Smithsonian's National Portrait Gallery in Washington, D.C. represent the most iconic actress of the 20th century.

Connecticut actress Meryl Streep has been nominated for more Oscars than Hepburn, but she has only won three at this writing. According to Hepburn's brother Bob, when Streep was a young actress, she dropped by the Hepburn house in Fenwick to see his sister. Katharine wasn't home, so Bob entertained Streep for a time. Katharine was furious when she found out that he had spent time with the young actress in her absence in her home. One can only guess as to why she felt that way.

Hepburn remains an icon because of her brash, irreverent nature. She demanded, and received, respect. Her fashion style also remains legendary. Her high-waisted trousers stood for independence. In Hepburn's era, actresses didn't dress that way, but she did. I think she knew they made her look taller, though she wasn't short at just over 5 feet 7 inches.

She received such attention in the 1920s when she first arrived in Hollywood because she was different from all the rest of the women who were shooting for the stars. She was a New England beauty with a lock-jawed affluent accent, the likes of which hadn't often been seen before. She was strong-willed, independent, and went after what she wanted no matter what the cost. Along the way Hollywood learned to

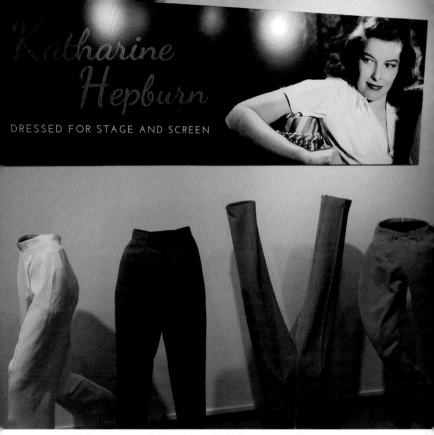

Kate's famous pants on display—she was ahead of her time.

deal with her, especially when she became a moneymaker. She made more than fifty films over the course of her career.

Hepburn was a workaholic her entire life. She's on record as saying she would have been a terrible mother because there would have been no time for little ones. Though, as you will find out in the pages to come, she looked out for and "mothered" many people.

Hepburn's Ties to Connecticut

Katharine Hepburn loved Connecticut and was good to it. The southern New England enclave of Fenwick (a borough by the sea in Old Saybrook) was her retreat during her golden days in Hollywood and times in between. It gave her comfort. But she often brought Hollywood to Fenwick—movie stars and producers, authors and playwrights came to call. Many showed up to spend time with her in her rather secluded mansion by the sea.

Hepburn preferred privacy and her beloved community fiercely protected that desire right up until the end of her days and, to certain degrees, even now, even though she is gone. When I talk to people who knew her, they tell me stories but there is always a sense that there are other things they know but hold back out of respect for her.

Hepburn loved the color red, she wore it all the time. Perhaps she knew it was a "power" color. When the Katharine Hepburn Cultural Arts Center in Old Saybrook was built, the foundation was mindful of all of Hepburn's "likes." They took great care in developing a place that would suit its namesake. It is a living museum to her and they are mindful of that everyday. As a nod to her love of the color, the chairs in The Kate, as it is known, are red.

I am a television news reporter, a storyteller, and decades ago at WTNH-TV (ABC) in New Haven, Connecticut, I desperately wanted an interview with Hepburn. A coworker, Kevin Hogan, gave me her brother Bob's phone number. Bob, in turn gave me Kate's number in New York City. The face-to-face interview never panned out, but I did talk to her by phone from her home in Turtle Bay. The icon herself picked up the phone after a few rings . . . what a thrill that was. I remember our short chat like it was yesterday. She told me she wouldn't talk to me on camera because I would never be able to "light her properly." She told me that only the crew who worked with Barbara Walters could do that. She had done a television interview with Walters and apparently she had liked how she was "lit." I have this conversation on audiotape. Even after she told me "no," I persisted in a true Hepburn way. I think I said I would send her flowers or some such nervous reply, alas she hung up and that was the end of that, but

the brush with Hepburn has stayed with me. I did correspond with her secretary Sharon Powers over the years, trying to persuade her into an interview, but it never happened. I do, however, have the correspondence on Katharine Hepburn stationary framed on a wall in my home. It's one of my prized possessions.

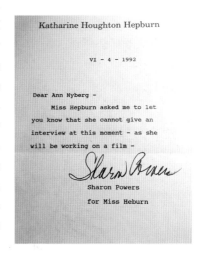

Katharine Houghton Hepburn

VI - 4 - 1992

Dear Ann Nyberg -
    Miss Hepburn asked me to let you know that she cannot give an interview at this moment - as she will be working on a film -

Sharon Powers

for Miss Heburn

A Legend Lost

Hepburn died in 2003 at the age of ninety-six at her Fenwick home. Though she is gone, countless stories are still being written about her every day. In this book, you will read stories about her days in Hollywood from those who knew her best and from her family, too.

I explore untold stories of the legendary actress from folks who knew her and people who have interviewed her over the years, including Dick Cavett who snagged the first television interview with her.

I wanted to talk to anybody who could give me different perspectives on this icon. I spent time in her home in Fenwick to see what she saw as she spent decades on those grounds by the sea, watching the sun rise and set from the time she was a little girl until her death there. I wanted to know who Hepburn was, what made her tick, did she ever let her guard down, what was she thinking in her most private moments?

These stories paint a picture and offer a glimpse into the world of a Hollywood legend, a woman whom I have always admired.

A Note from the Author

A documentary called *A Star Among Us* was produced and directed by former Katharine Hepburn Cultural Arts Center founding trustee Bob Czepiel. My interviews are included in this film; this is the first time they are in print. *A Star Among Us* plays at The Kate, and is a great source of information on Hepburn.

While I can transcribe all the wonderful interviews I had with the people who knew Hepburn, the one thing I can't get across in writing is the wonderful way many of these people related their stories to me. I truly wish you could have been there with me to witness the nuances from the likes of Sam Waterston, Anthony Harvey, and Norah Moore who could all do a "spot on" Hepburn voice.

fenwick antics

The Hepburns bought a summer home in Fenwick, a borough located in Old Saybrook, Connecticut, 50 miles south of Hartford, in 1912. Fenwick was a kind of Victorian commune, formed in the 1870s by mostly elite families from Hartford who built large, shingled cottages. It is a tiny peninsula facing Long Island Sound, with the Connecticut River on its eastern boundary and the South Cove on its western side.

The house was as close to the water as one could get, a rambling three-story place with twelve or more rooms; a wide front porch; peaks; gables; and, originally, one bathroom. Here, Katharine spent most of her childhood summers. She was excellent in swimming, diving, and golf. The four swings on the porch and the spooky "secret passages" in the third-floor attic fascinated the children of Fenwick. Kate and her brother Dick put on plays like *Beauty and the Beast* and *Bluebeard*.

Fenwick (2016)

In 1937, after his junior year at Harvard, Ellsworth Grant planned to drive to California with two of his classmates, Tom Calhoun and Caspar Weinberger (future US Secretary of Defense under President Ronald Regan), but first he had to say goodbye his serious girlfriend, Marion Hepburn, who was at her family's home in Fenwick. He remembers arriving on a Saturday afternoon. Marion and her mother were waiting for them, while Katharine was expected later from New York with a new beau.

He lets Tom Calhoun tell the rest of the story in his own words:

After dinner, Marion and Ellsworth went for a walk on the beach. Caspar and I were put into a guest bedroom. There was a bathroom between our room and another guest room. Caspar said he would take a shower and go to bed. I was listening to Caspar singing in the shower about the girl of his dreams when a loud banging commenced on the bathroom door, which was then accompanied by someone screaming, "Who the hell is using that shower?"

> "I HAVE LOVED AND BEEN IN LOVE. THERE'S A BIG DIFFERENCE."
> —katharine hepburn

There was silence as the shower water hissed to a whisper and Caspar's surprised reply came through the wall. "It is I, Caspar."

"I don't care who you are, the angry female yelled. "Get out of there! That's Howard's shower!"

The next minute the doors to the hall and the bathroom flew open at the same time. Through one dashed Caspar with a towel around his waist. Through the other came a tall, thin, redheaded girl with fire in her green eyes.

"The Howard" in question was Katharine's current beau, Howard Hughes, the eccentric, famous flyer, for whom she had a new bathroom built especially so he wouldn't be exposed to other people's germs. That night he failed to show up, but arrived the next day in his seaplane, this was the most dramatic event in Fenwick's history except for the hurricane of 1938. The family was glad when the romance ended, as he had been a difficult and demanding guest.

Ellsworth Grant recalled: September 21, 1938, dawned bright in the borough of Fenwick, Old Saybrook, at the mouth of the Connecticut River. Most of the summer residents had closed their houses after Labor Day, but the Hepburn family had stayed on. Katharine was elated that her new play, *The Philadelphia Story,* was headed for Broadway. She took her usual early morning swim and played a round of golf on the nine-hole course. The wind began to rise on the par-three ninth hole and her ball flew straight for the hole. Her first hole-in-one and a record 31 strokes!

After four days of heavy rains the weather was very warm and muggy. At 2:00 p.m., the rain fell again in torrents. Soon a gigantic wall of black-green salt water smashed against the shores of Connecticut,

After the Hurricane of 1938.

Rhode Island, and Massachusetts. The ocean tides, already at their fullest flood because of the autumnal equinox, rose 10 to 17 feet above normal. Nine bodies washed ashore in Westbrook.

As the storm gathered strength that morning, Mrs. Thomas Hepburn was reading the latest play by George Bernard Shaw, her favorite author. Nothing could disturb her concentration. But her daughter, her son, Dick, an aspiring playwright; Jack Hammond, Dick's college friend; and their old nurse Fanny were increasingly alarmed as the water rose, windows blew in, and the wind howled louder than ever before. They were used to severe storms from the southwest, but this morning was different.

> "LIFE CAN BE WILDLY TRAGIC AT TIMES, AND I'VE HAD MY SHARE. BUT WHATEVER HAPPENS TO YOU, YOU HAVE TO KEEP A SLIGHTLY COMIC ATTITUDE. IN THE FINAL ANALYSIS, YOU HAVE GOT NOT TO FORGET TO LAUGH."
>
> —katharine hepburn

Mrs. Hepburn pooh-poohed their concerns. "Call Stanley," she said, "and have him come board up the windows." As soon as the carpenter arrived, his Model A Ford blew over the lagoon on the north side of the house. A shell-shocked casualty of World War I, he was in no condition to repair windows.

By then the water had risen over the windowsills. Dick finally convinced his mother this was no ordinary storm and led them out through a window. He had to carry Fanny, who weighed about 200 pounds. As they reached higher ground, they looked back. The house suddenly disintegrated. In Hepburn's autobiography she recalled: "It just sailed away as easy as pie and soon there was nothing at all left. Our house—ours for twenty-five years—all our possessions just gone. My God, it was something devastating and real, like the beginning of the world—or the end of it."

Everything was gone, except for the third floor, which serenely floated east toward the Connecticut River. The next morning they found the floor intact with Dick's typewriter and latest manuscript still on the desk.

Some of the summer residents had left behind a few servants to close up their homes for the winter. When the worst has passed, Katharine gathered the frightened domestics and took them to the closed River Sea Inn for the night. Candles provided the only light. Just as she settled down, she had the good sense to see that every candle had been extinguished. Sure enough in the hall she found one about to topple over that might have set the whole place on fire.

Katharine spent the next few days digging among the ruins of the Hepburn cottage, recovering some of the family silver. Without delay, she and her father, Dr. Hepburn, decided to build a much larger brick home on the same spot. He was heard to exclaim: "I'll not let old Neptune get the better of me!"

Looking for valuables lost in the Hurricane of 1938.

One of Dick Hepburn's children, Mundy, told Old Saybrook native Viola Tagliatela that during the Hurricane of 1938, Hepburn attempted to go back to get a gold clock given to her by Howard Hughes, whom she dated and who is also credited for helping Hepburn get back on her feet after some box office flops. The clock had a pendulum, which contained a huge emerald, but according to Mundy, Hepburn ended up abandoning it to get herself and her mother to safety. Tagliatela believes that clock could still be under the foundation to this day. However, the home has been lifted and the ground beneath it dug up, and no word surfaced that the clock was ever found. Perhaps it was swept out to sea in the storm.

Woman of the Year (1942) with Spencer Tracy.

Ellsworth Grant recalled: One summer in 1946, after World War II, when my family still occupied the west wing of Katharine's new Fenwick house, Spencer Tracy came for a weekend. As was the case with Howard Hughes, there were frantic last-minute preparations. A coffeemaker had to be placed beside his bed so he could have his brews immediately upon waking.

As the clan gathered for dinner Saturday night, a typical southwesterly storm was building. Angry waves pounded against the Fenwick pier and the Hepburn breakwaters. The little fleet of Indian-class sailboats bounced around in the harbor and strained at their moorings. Katharine looked out the window and cried, "Off with your pants!"

Spencer looked stupefied while Dick, Bob, and I stripped to our shorts and rushed out into the night. The crisis calling for such drastic action was a boat that had broken loose and was about to crash on the rocky beach. We hauled it to safety and returned dripping. Spencer looked at us in disbelief and said, "You're all mad!"

Norah Moore was Katharine Hepburn's cook for more than three decades. She remembers when she didn't have something such as the star's favorite brownies ready to eat when she wanted them, Hepburn would yell, "Norah!" and would then come into the kitchen. When that happened, it wasn't a good thing, because that would lead to Norah having a rough day on the job. Norah says cooks don't need somebody else stepping into the kitchen and fouling things up, which is what would happen if Hepburn was there with her. Two cooks in her kitchen just didn't work.

Norah Moore (left) with her daughter and granddaughter.

Norah worked for Hepburn in New York and in Fenwick. She says the phone never stopped ringing at Hepburn's townhouse in Turtle Bay. She said along with the role of cook, she also served as a secretary, moving at a feverish pace most of the time. The two were friends, though, until the end of Hepburn's life. It is written that in Hepburn's will, she left Norah $200,000.

As a teenager and into her twenties, Old Saybrook native Viola Tagliatela spent a lot of time at Katharine Hepburn's summer "cottage" in Fenwick. Her then-boyfriend "Rock" was studying theater directing with famed Broadway director, Word Baker. (Baker was a director who, in 1960, set *The Fantasticks* spinning into theater history as the world's longest-running musical.) It just so happened that Baker had been invited by Hepburn to stay at her mansion. Because Rock and Baker commuted "hither and yon together," it was just easier if Rock lived in the Hepburn house, too. Though Rock's apartment was private, with its own small kitchen, living room, and bedroom suite, he still had total access to the rest of the home.

You start to get the feeling that the Hepburn place in the star's later years was like a boarding house. Tagliatela says the house was partitioned off for other immediate members of Hepburn's family to live there and be comfortable. Hepburn's brother Dick was living in the home at the time with his wife and kids. In fact, Hepburn's nieces and nephews were another reason Tagliatela was in the Hepburn home so much. She was good friends with Ky and Ailee Hepburn, two of Dick Hepburn's four children.

Tagliatela graduated from high school in 1976, and spent many hours at the Hepburn place with her friends. She noted that Kate's nieces and nephews referred to actor Spencer Tracy, the love of Hepburn's life, as "Uncle Spencer." This could lead one to believe that perhaps Tracy spent time at the summer cottage with the family along the way, though no one knows for sure how much time.

According to Tagliatela, Hepburn would stay in Fenwick on weekends and during the week would travel to Turtle Bay in New York City where she would entertain the rich and the famous.

Tagliatela found the actress to be very pleasant and insightful, often taking time to chat with her. She marveled that Hepburn put up with so many teenagers together in one house with all the noise they made and their comings and goings. She remembered stopping to talk to Hepburn who was arranging flowers in the kitchen.

"Do you know why I am doing this with the flowers?" Hepburn asked her, and then went on to explain. "You must take the leaves off so the flowers will last longer. You cut the bottom of the flower at a slant so it will get the appropriate amount of water."

Tagliatela was so taken aback that Hepburn would take the time to explain something to a teenager who may or may not have cared. She said Hepburn was always in the large kitchen fixing something and preferred to eat in. She remembered Hepburn remarking that eating out was ridiculous because it was a real waste of money. She heard her say, "If you all want to go out, give me the money you would spend, or go out and get the groceries and I will cook the dinner."

Tagliatela said Kate was sensible and didn't spend money on what she thought were frivolous items. Though she said the Hepburn family did not "want for things," and were well taken care of.

Hepburn was extremely casual at home. She would wear a sweatshirt and sweatpants around the house, a far cry from the fashionista status she developed in Old Hollywood. At home Kate just wanted to be comfortable.

Jack Daniel Rehm's father and a man named Charlie Mallard were college roommates and very good friends. Charlie introduced JD's father to a man named Chris Barrett, who in turn introduced him to bucolic Fenwick in the 1960s. I relate all this to provide a picture of how things go in Fenwick; everything is very connected and all about community. Everybody knows everybody and summertime is paradise with sailing and swimming and suppers together all over the borough.

Fenwick is a very tight-knit place, and if you're not "all in" you miss out on a lot. Generation after generation of families know each other, the kids have all grown up together, and some have married, some in a small chapel in the enclave called Saint-Mary's-By-The-Sea. Part of the chapel was built in 1887, and it blends right into the shingled homes and has a bell tower. If only the walls could talk.

JD Rehm's family started summer life in the enclave in the 1960s as renters, initially just for the month of July, then for July and August, and then, in 1981, JD's parents bought in hook, line, and sinker and became Fenwick homeowners. The family still owns that home and now JD and his family, including his wife, daughter of Charlie Mallard, have their own home and continue their summers there. The Fenwick circle of life continues.

JD sums up Fenwick in this way: "When you go there you say, this place is beautiful, it has beautiful homes, it's on the water, how bucolic, how beautiful. But the reality is, it is a community and that's what is at its core. We all care for each other. We all look out for not only each other, but for Fenwick, because we care so much about

Pat and Mike (1952).

preserving it. We all volunteer, we all get involved with different committees to make sure that Fenwick is well taken care of, not only for today, but for tomorrow as well."

> "I NEVER LOSE SIGHT OF THE FACT THAT JUST BEING IS FUN."
> —katharine hepburn

He immensely enjoys his time in Fenwick and remembers often seeing Hepburn buzzing around the community on her bike or golf cart (the vehicle of choice in Fenwick). He was never star-struck, he said. All the kids knew she was a celebrity, but he was two generations removed, she wasn't a star of his time.

When JD Rehm was about ten years old, he was on Fenwick beach near Katharine Hepburn's home when a catamaran pulled up to her shore. He and his young friend were invited to go sailing. Fenwick, for kids, was and is, full of adventure and this was just another day there. At the helm was Hepburn's brother Dick and some of his friends. JD can't believe his parents let him do this, but off they went, he and his friend, on the boat, which hugged the Connecticut shoreline to Essex. Once they got to the small coastal town, the whole lot of them were picked up by Katharine Hepburn in her Lincoln Town Car. He remembers thinking that there was no way they would all fit, but somehow they did. They all squished in and sat on each other's laps and all the doors got shut. Off to Fenwick they went, driving down the road with Hepburn behind the wheel. This was young JD's first introduction to Hepburn.

He says even in his younger days, he really did have affection for her, realizing all she had accomplished in her life. He started watching her movies, going to Thursday night screenings at her brother-in-law's house down the way from Hepburn's place. He remembers everybody heading into Ellsworth Grant's screening room at the back of the house. This was just something you did during the summer in Fenwick. He never saw Hepburn when he was there, though he knew she made frequent stops there visiting her sister Marion and Ellsworth and their kids.

He remembers wanting her to live forever because of all of the memories he had of her. He says, "I liked her, I found her to be a sweet woman, sweet in that she treated me well, even though she didn't care about learning about me, she treated me well. She was always a pleasure to interact with. I'm sure she did ask me questions, I just can't remember, but it wasn't anything that was monumental at the time."

One summer when JD Rehm was about sixteen or seventeen, he, his sister, and some friends ran into Katharine Hepburn on the beach near her home. A sailboat offshore seemed to her to be in some kind of trouble. She always kept a watchful eye on what was going on in the waters around her home. She thought those on board needed some help. Hepburn yelled to JD's sister, "Take this canoe, take this canoe! This was Hank's gift to me!" In later years, they realized that the canoe in which they started paddling out to help the sailboat was the very one used in the movie *On Golden Pond,* and "Hank" was the one and only Henry Fonda, who wanted Hepburn to have the canoe after filming the movie.

JD says that in looking back he realized she referenced the connection to the movie to the kids because she wanted them to know its worth. This was a glimpse into her world as a movie star. As it turned, the sailboat was not in distress and it was much ado about nothing . . . but there they were at the mouth of the Connecticut River looking back at Hepburn's mansion on the sea in that canoe given to her by Fonda.

One day in July of 1980, JD was playing tennis on one of the four Fenwick courts with a friend. Hepburn was playing on the next court over. She was into her seventies by this time, but still lobbing the ball in fine fashion. JD's court time was up, and he and his partner were leaving to make room for the next twosome coming on. As they were leaving, Hepburn called out, "Would you two like to play with us?" JD and his friend said, "Sure!" and a doubles match ensued.

JD was Hepburn's partner and he remembers they played for about forty-five minutes. His friend's partner was a Hollywood movie director, but he can't remember which one. At the Hepburn home the famous were constantly coming and going and Fenwick just took that all in stride.

This doubles match began a partnership for JD and Hepburn. He remembers her playing with an oversized-head metal Prince racquet. JD thought the racquet was so odd looking. Hepburn was one of the first to use such a racquet, and he thought she was cheating with it. When JD asked her why she was using it, she told him that when he got to be her age, he too would want to play with a racquet like hers. She played well into her seventies if not her eighties, and JD says she never gave up and she was just "incredible." Hepburn would ring him up week after week for two months to play tennis. JD admits he was a darn good player, and Hepburn, quite the athlete, always loved a challenge.

"She never got cross with me, I mean I was late, twenty or thirty minutes late sometimes for our tennis matches and she would never say, "Excuse me, young man, you know we had a date at 4:00, it's 4:30. Where are you? No, she just went with it."

He remembers one day as he approached her to play on the courts, she was reading something. He asked her what it was and she told him it was a script for a movie with Henry Fonda called *On Golden Pond.* You don't hear *that* everyday! He believes it was that fall that she started filming the Academy Award–winning movie. It would be her last motion picture. Looking back on the summer, JD says he is so glad that he has these stories to tell. Indeed he played tennis with one of the most iconic actresses on the planet.

Fenwick (2016)

On the set of *Guess Who's Coming to Dinner?* (1967)

Viola Tagliatela has lived in the bucolic seaside town of Old Saybrook since she was two years old. Her parents moved to town in 1960, and she has lasting memories of Katharine Hepburn. She told me she first encountered Hepburn when she was about eleven years old. A lover of animals, Viola was riding her pony, Shiloh, down Maple Avenue. Shiloh had been a regular in town for eighteen years. On this particular day, Hepburn, then in her sixties and her brother Richard "Dick," were out for a bike ride around town. According to Viola, when they came upon her astride Shiloh, Hepburn left the sidewalk and went around her on her bike, saying in that world-famous voice, "I will honor your right of way" and just kept on going.

Hepburn wanted to make sure Viola and her pony could mosey along without Hepburn getting in the way. Imagine that? Hepburn gave her a very pleasant smile, and Viola thought the gesture was very kind.

Most folks in Old Saybrook were honored that Katharine Hepburn lived among them and they treated her with respect and gave her great privacy. In fact, the town closed ranks around her, protecting her at all costs from outsiders. At a young age Viola knew there was a famous actress living in her small town, but she had no idea then how iconic she was. It wasn't until she was much older, when someone explained how famous Hepburn was, that she got the whole picture. Before that, Viola just knew her as a neighbor.

When outsiders would run into Hepburn in town, Viola said, they would "do stupid things." For instance, she remembers one time she saw a woman put her ice cream cone into her own pocketbook upon the sight of Hepburn at James Pharmacy and Soda Fountain! For the townspeople, however, seeing the star at this local hangout was nothing unusual. As a teenager Tagliatela remembers having short conversations with the film icon at the counter. One day Hepburn told her she must read a book called *Nop's Trials* by Donald McCaig about a border collie who had hardships in life. As to not disappoint Hepburn when she saw her again, Viola went out and got the book and read it. When she saw Hepburn again she was able to report back to her on what she thought about it. Viola isn't sure whether Hepburn just liked the book or whether there was some life lesson to be learned from it. That was the Hepburn she came to know, always teaching people things.

Circa 1946.

Since 1960, Walt's Food Market on Main Street in Old Saybrook has been an institution in town. As you might guess, their most famous customer was Katharine Hepburn. Paul Kozey, son of owner Walter Kozey, remembers a time when Hepburn ordered leg of lamb and stated that they "should hurry and get it for her." It didn't matter if the shop was full of people, employees should just drop what they were doing and fill her order. With her standing there, they pretty much did just that—hopped to it and got her what she wanted so she could be on her way. It's just the way it was.

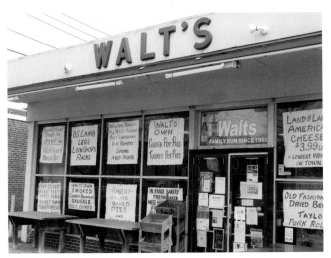

Walt's Food Market

The building in which the James Pharmacy and Soda
Fountain in Old Saybrook is located dates to 1790. The pharmacy was founded in 1917 by Anna Louise James, the first African-American female pharmacist in Connecticut. Ms. James ran her place until 1967. The building and business has gone through changes throughout the years, but there is still a counter there where customers order ice cream and milk shakes. Katharine Hepburn was known to frequent the establishment during her time in Fenwick.

Former owner and pharmacist Garth Meadows recalls stories of the historic place. Meadows syas one time when Hepburn was around nineteen years old, she was at the counter talking to Miss James. Miss James asked her why she looked so down in the dumps. Hepburn said

James Pharmacy and Soda Fountain

there was a part in a play opening in New York City that she had her heart set on. She wanted to audition but she needed bus fare. She explained that her parents wouldn't give it to her because she didn't have their permission to go.

Miss James thought about her predicament and went into a back room for a minute. When she came out, she plunked the needed money down on the counter for Hepburn. She said, "There you go, you take that bus and you go down and give it your best shot."

Hepburn went and landed the part in the play, though Meadows doesn't know what the play or the role was. That just may have been the start of her career. Miss James played a part in helping Hepburn become the megastar she turned out to be.

"With Miss Hepburn there was no grey area, ever," says former Old Saybrook police detective Gene Heiney, who respected Hepburn to her very core. Heiney grew up on the "other side of the causeway" from Fenwick, in the main part of town, but spent a lot of time during his childhood in the bucolic borough because his best friend was Hepburn's nephew, Tor. Hepburn's brother Dick lived with her in the big house with his family, so this was a kind of headquarters for Gene. He chuckles when he thinks about hanging out in the home of one of the most famous actresses of all time. To him, though, "Miss Hepburn" was just Tor's aunt. He didn't really think of her as a big deal, at least not then. Later in life he would come to understand her huge celebrity. Toward the end of her life, as a police officer he protected her privacy at all costs in the home in which he had spent so much time as a child.

As Gene tells it, after school he would take the bus with Tor to Fenwick. Or sometimes his mom or dad would drop him off at the Hepburn house, driving past that sign that said, "Please go away" (put up for tourists who would come gawking and want to see her house or try to catch a glimpse of her).

He said as a kid he found the Hepburn house to be quite cluttered, full of stuff, and a place of wonderful childhood experiences. "To me it was just huge."

Hepburn's Fenwick home was situated at the mouth of the Connecticut River and Long Island Sound. Tor and Gene used to swim off her beach a lot. "We would go running out the back door of her house and right into Long Island Sound," he remembers. "One day in her kitchen, when I was over at the house as a kid, she chased me around with a wooden spoon. I had just said a swear word and she did not like that one bit and she was going to teach me not to do that again. I don't know what I said, but she was chasing me around the kitchen table. She was very big on manners, period."

He says after he grew up, he lost touch with the Hepburn family a bit until he became a member of the police force in town as a detective. The relationship picked right back up from where it had started when he was a kid.

Gene remembers the time when Hepburn decided to leave her townhouse in Turtle Bay, New York, to come home to Fenwick to live out the rest of her days in the place she called her "paradise." That's where his caretaking of Hepburn began.

He says the Hepburn family contacted him, as did one of her co-executors, Erik Hanson, who was Hepburn's accountant and friend. The other executor was then ABC News correspondent Cynthia McFadden, a long-time, close friend of Hepburn's.

Gene was asked to come up with a plan that would be implemented on the day of her passing, one that would pay total respect to her. He knew that day would be a huge deal. He wanted to do his best to keep the press away from her home and from Fenwick, otherwise it would turn into a media free-for-all. At all costs he was going to see to it that Hepburn and her family had their privacy at the end no matter what.

"I went down to the house to make all the arrangements for the future, and I even met with her [Hepburn]. She was doing pretty well at the time; she was well into her nineties," said Gene. "I did a security survey of the house to figure out how best everything could be carried out.

Through the time that Gene was making arrangements, he often visited the Fenwick mansion. "There were good days and bad days for her at the end," he said. "I won't forget one conversation I had with her at the house, it has stuck with me.

"She started calling me Mr. Heiney. That's just the way she was, very proper. She reminded me a lot of my grandmother. She was an old swamp Yankee and that was it, you were not going to change her mind. Swamp Yankees are thrifty and steadfast and what was right was right, period.

"I was called to go down to the Hepburn house one day because she was having some medical issues. I barged right in. I found Ms. Hepburn sitting on a couch and her driver was with her. He told me she was having trouble breathing, but that she was refusing to go to the clinic. I sat down next to her and started talking to her and she just kind of shrugged her shoulders. I thought to myself, *She is digging in her heels and we're going to have a battle here to get her to leave the house to go get checked out.*"

Gene said he understood her stubbornness, so he knew the kind of tactic he would take to get her out of the house.

"I said, 'How are you feeling?' and took her hand. She told me she was having a little trouble breathing, but said, 'I'm NOT going anywhere, this is my home.'"

About this time the ambulance arrived. I asked the EMTs to leave for a minute so I could continue to persuade her that she would need to have some medical attention elsewhere. The team left for a time, but it wasn't long before trouble started.

"One of the paramedics came back into the room. He was chomping gum to beat the band, which got Hepburn's attention and that's when the antics started. He knelt down in front of her as she was sitting on the couch. He was really going to town on his gum, which was so rude. Katharine is getting worse, not breathing very well by this time. I was leaning over her and holding her hand. The guy with the gum starts talking to her saying, 'Miss Hepburn, how do you feel?' and on and on and on. Asking all the paramedic questions while his mouth is going with the gum. Hepburn looks up at me, she didn't move her head, she just looked up at me with her eyes and I thought, *Uh-oh, something's coming; she is going to blow her top.* Sure enough, she ripped into that guy like there was no tomorrow."

"Young man," started Hepburn. "When you're in the presence of a lady, you don't chew gum. Now get out of my house!"

"The guy looks up at me," Gene says, "and I tell him, 'Yeah, you better leave.' He says, 'Are you kidding?' I said, 'No, just get out, go out into the other room.'"

"I sat down with Miss Hepburn and her driver. There were a couple of other people there by then from the family. 'Miss Hepburn,' I said. 'You really have to go to the clinic, you're having trouble breathing.' She thought about what I said for a moment and, as if she was on a stage, made an announcement to everybody in the room.

"Mr. Heiney says I have to go to the clinic. I'm going to the clinic, but I don't want that young man with the gum anywhere near me."

Gene made sure that EMT was banished from the trip to the clinic. He says, "I'll never forget when she looked at me with that I'll-show-him-who's-boss twinkle in her eye concerning the guy with the gum. That was a look when you just knew some verbal assault was about to be thrown down, I wasn't sure just what it would be, but it was always delivered from her with a blow."

The Iron Petticoat (1956)

[Katharine Hepburn] was just wonderful, but just really normal. To me she was just Aunt Kate. To most others she was an icon. To me she was just a normal, down-to-earth gal. There was no grey area with her, she either liked you or she didn't.

As a kid growing up, I knew her to be very private. I used to see her riding her bike into town, that's how everybody knew her. She would stop and have a conversation with my father in the yard and then she would be on her way to run errands or whatever. She would always tell him if he needed anything to get a hold of her staff at the house.

— Gene Heiney, childhood friend to Hepburn's nephew, Tor

When Old Saybrook police detective Gene Heiney was on the force, he and fellow officer Jerry Rankin would throw an old-fashioned lobster bake on the beach for the department. To do it right, according to Heiney, you need a particular type of seaweed to throw over the food while it's cooking.

"We went down to the breakwater in Fenwick," remembers Heiney, "which is right in front of Katharine's house. It was about, oh I don't know, maybe 6:00 in the morning. It was low tide and I was dragging the bags of seaweed to the truck while Jerry was getting more. I looked back and there she was. Kate comes stormin' out of her house and walks down the yard. By this time I'm a quarter mile away. I'm watching her and thinking, *Oh boy my buddy's caught.* We didn't get permission from her. It was just one of those things where we always went down there for the seaweed every year.

> "TO KEEP YOUR CHARACTER INTACT YOU CANNOT STOOP TO FILTHY ACTS. IT MAKES IT EASIER TO STOOP THE NEXT TIME."
>
> —katharine hepburn

Well she starts rippin' into my buddy screaming, "Who do you think you are?!" She is shaking she is so angry.

"I'm from the police department," Jerry says. "I'm here with Gene Heiney."

The Philadelphia Story (1940)

She looks over to me and yells, "Do you know this young man?"

"Yes I do, Miss Hepburn," I say. "I'm sorry. We didn't want to wake you up."

She calms herself and says, "Okay, well come on in for a drink, then, when you're ready."

Gene says that's just the type of person she was, she would confront you and, if she didn't like you, would let you know that immediately. When she saw who was there on that early morning then it was fine. "The next year, though," Gene says, "we made sure to ask permission for the seaweed."

Kay Hall, a volunteer at the Katharine Hepburn Cultural Arts Center (The Kate) in Old Saybrook moved to town in 1970 and fell in love with its surroundings. From time to time she would see Katharine Hepburn riding around town on her bicycle, wearing a large hat, scarf, and sunglasses, which was Hepburn's usual outfit when she went out and about riding.

One day Kay was playing golf on the public, nine-hole course in Fenwick as part of an outing for R.R. Donnelley & Sons, a now closed printing plant in town. Her daughter Meredith, who was perhaps in fifth grade at the time, needed to find her for one reason or another. She took her bike and rolled over to nearby Fenwick and started riding up and down the fairways trying to find her mom.

About this time Hepburn, who lived right near the golf course, had gotten a glimpse of this child riding about in a forbidden way on a golf course. She decided to flag her down and give her a lesson on what not to do on a golf course.

This is the way Meredith remembers what happened:

A woman came out of her house with a hat and sunglasses and said to me, "Little girl you shouldn't be riding on the fairways like this."

Meredith didn't quite know at the time who was scolding her, but quickly figured it out. She had seen the movie *African Queen* in which Hepburn starred, and the light bulb went off. She told Hepburn she was looking for her mom, to which Hepburn said, "Well, you can't ride in the fairways because you're going to get hit by a ball."

Meredith persisted and said, "I just want to find my mom; she's playing golf." Hall admits that her daughter, even at a young age, was pretty outgoing. Meredith then asked Hepburn if she played golf.

Hepburn said, "Yes I do, but I prefer tennis."

Meredith told her that her mom played tennis too.

As Hall tells it, the two of them had a nice long conversation on the golf course. We suppose by now that Hepburn had gotten her out of the way of any would-be flying balls. Hall believes by that time her daughter was walking her bike as the two strolled and talked out of harm's way.

Hall says her daughter went home and forgot all about her or why she needed her in the first place. After all, she had just spent time with that lady she had seen in a movie.

Back in the day when Old Saybrook resident Sharon Baldie was in high school, an aging Hepburn was spending a lot of time in her beloved town. Baldie knew of Hepburn as a child because she had been to the Fenwick house for birthday parties for her friend Ailee, Hepburn's niece. One day during her senior year, Baldie was leaving basketball practice. It was right around dinnertime and it was snowing to beat the band. When she got out to the parking lot, she discovered her car wouldn't start. Since this was long before cell phones, the thing that occurred to Baldie to do was to go out to the road in front of the high school and try to flag down a driver to get her home.

By this time she couldn't see at all, the flakes were coming down fast and furious, it was a white out. She only lived about a mile and a half away and figured standing there on the road somebody who knew her would certainly stop and pick her up. Old Saybrook is a small town and residents generally knew each other. Baldie, who is a tiny thing, about 5 feet, 1 inch tall, stuck her thumb right out there in the blinding snow and hoped for the best. She describes the weather as a down-right blizzard. She started to think that since it was so bad out, maybe no one would be out driving. But someone was. The driver behind the wheel of the first car to stop was Katharine Hepburn.

Driving really slow, Hepburn pulls right over in her big car. By this time, there was nearly 8 inches or so of heavy, wet snow on the ground with no signs of it letting up. Hepburn rolled down the window, and said, "Get in." That's when Baldie got her first glimpse of who her chauffeur was. As she recognized the driver, she was both

On the set of *Bringing Up Baby* (1938)

horrified and so very, very grateful all at the same time. She just wanted to get out of the elements as fast as she could.

She knew it was Hepburn but didn't want to let on that she knew it was *her*. As a teenager she was so embarrassed by what was happening. She didn't really know how to handle all of the emotions going on—the car not starting, the snowstorm, and the fact that an iconic actress who really shouldn't even be on the road at her age was about to take her home. Never mind the fact that if her dad found out she had been hitchhiking, well that would lead to trouble too. Her dad had two rules in their household: One, don't ever get on a motorcycle and; two, never, ever hitchhike.

Baldie hopped into the front seat alongside Hepburn and there they were, the two of them. Baldie says so much was running through her head. What should she say to the star? Should she talk to her? She didn't want to talk out of turn. Should she say something first? Would Hepburn? She was even afraid to make eye contact with the star, she didn't want her to think she was staring at her. Should she look straight ahead or maybe out the window? This was nerve-wracking stuff!

Here she was, sitting in the car in her basketball get up—her letterman jacket, sneakers, and all—hardly dressed for the snow. Baldie, nervously started to talk. Telling Hepburn first that her car wouldn't start, then thanking her for stopping to get her, never letting on that she knew she was talking to *the* Katharine Hepburn.

"I just live off of Pennywise Lane," Baldie said very quickly and nervously. "I didn't want to call my parents, because of the bad weather. I thought this would be easy, that I could just get a quick ride home and not have to bother them." She was trying to play it cool. As if this was just one townsperson talking to another Old Saybrookian. Then she just stopped talking, she didn't know what to do next. She was frozen, literally, and, by this time, physically shaking.

By now they were headed to Baldie's house, the car going ever so slowly, excruciatingly slow, she thinks maybe 5 miles an hour if that. The weather was that bad, clearly no one should have been on the roads. Still there had been no words from Hepburn. This was to be the longest mile-and-a-half ride Baldie would have in her life.

They finally got to the top of Baldie's road. She turned to Hepburn and said, "Ms. Hepburn, thank you very much, but please don't tell my father I was hitchhiking because he will kill me, that just isn't allowed." She doesn't even know why she told her that, because Hepburn would have no way of knowing her dad, but as a teenager that's just the kind of thing you say.

"KINDNESS IS ONE OF THE GREATEST GIFTS YOU CAN BESTOW UPON ANOTHER. IF SOMEONE IS IN NEED, LEND THEM A HELPING HAND. DO NOT WAIT FOR A THANK YOU. TRUE KINDNESS LIES WITHIN THE ACT OF GIVING WITHOUT THE EXPECTATION OF SOMETHING IN RETURN." —katharine hepburn

Finally Hepburn spoke after all that time and said very slowly, "Oh, don't worry; it's okay."

Again, Baldie thanked Hepburn profusely for helping her get home and then went on to tell her that she was a friend of her niece, Ailee, as if to let her know that the person she just gave a ride to was okay because she knew a family member. Hepburn was glad to know the two were friends at the high school. Baldie then finally told Hepburn who she was. "I'm Sharon Baldie." She was thinking that Hepburn might go home and tell Ailee that she had just met her. She knew she wouldn't remember her being over at the house when she was much younger for birthday parties.

Hepburn then said, "Do you want me to bring you right to your house? We're only at the top of your street."

Baldie knew this would be trouble. If her parents saw a strange car driving up their driveway, they might find out she had been hitchhiking. That would be the worst scenario ever. She would rather they just believed that she walked all the way home.

Baldie finally told her parents many years later what had happened on that snowy evening. It had been her brush with greatness as experienced by a very nervous teenager.

The Gengras family goes way back in the fabled place called Fenwick. Skip Gengras's folks had a place in the borough that you see as you enter the causeway that links the main town of Old Saybrook and the borough. It's a magnificent place, with water views galore; that's where he spent his summers. Skip says his childhood in Fenwick was beyond special.

"The enclave is a tight-knit community where everybody takes care of everybody else's children and all the adults see to each other too," said Skip. "This is a very casual place. You could literally walk out your door any day of the week with a bathing suit on and that was just fine.

Today Skip believes Fenwick is still all about the welfare of the children. "I don't think I could find in this world a nicer more congenial place to raise children with the opportunities of the water, the golf course, tennis courts, and learning experiences and that's been true forever." He says it is a place filled with "low-key Yankees." It has its own elected officials who oversee the borough of about one hundred homes.

Skip describes Katharine Hepburn as very gracious. While she could also be aloof to youngsters, she also often threw a dance party at her home, which the kids loved. Skip recalls going to one of these parties with Edie, who would one day become his wife. Edie also summered in Fenwick. As young kids they danced it up at the Hepburn home. One year they won the dance contest. As a prize, Hepburn handed them a piece of cinnamon toast. Odd, but that was the prize. They had been hoping for a trophy of some sort with her name on it, but toast appeared, just toast, which fell flat on them, but it was presented to them by Katharine Hepburn. Skip guesses they were about twelve years old or so at the time.

He remembers one time after being a golf caddy for Hepburn on the Fenwick course that he was not pleased with the amount of money, twenty-five cents, that she had given him for his efforts. As the story goes, he called her a "bad name" under his breath as he walked away with the miniscule amount of money she had given him. Hepburn overheard what he had said to her. When he got home from the golf outing, his father was standing at the door ready with a verbal reprimand. Being the tight community that it was, his father found out immediately what he had done, and made him walk straight over to her home to apologize to her face. Skip was dispatched and off he went. He said it all went well, she came to the door, he apologized, she said thanks, and that was that.

On the set of *Summertime* (1955)

family affairs

Ellsworth Grant recalled: June 12, 1939 was a perfect summer day. At noon, I was committed to marry Marion Hepburn on the lawn of 201 Bloomfield Avenue in Hartford. I had argued for a small wedding, but was brusquely outvoted by my father and Mrs. Hepburn, whom I now called Mama. They conspired to produce a blowout, inviting 600 guests for a reception and sit-down luncheon served impeccably by the Hartford Club. But to tell the truth, the wedding was Katharine's because it had to be held on a Monday, her off-day of performing *The Philadelphia Story.*

I passed a nervous morning playing chess with my best man Clippy Amory at my parents' home. I had six ushers, my roommates at Harvard. The bridesmaids were Katharine and Peg Hepburn. The well-known Hungarian photographer, Martin Munkacsi, took a lot of pictures, Luddy—Katharine's ex-husband—was busy with his movie camera, and *Life* magazine had also sent a photographer.

Katharine, Peg, and Marion Hepburn (1939)

The minister was a gentle Unitarian minister, father of my usher Caleb Foote. Overwhelmed by the occasion, his legs shook during the ceremony.

For an hour, maybe two, the wedding party stood in line shaking hands. Everyone, of course, wanted to greet Katharine, who maintained a frozen smile beneath a large hat. After lunch she slipped away, and Marion and I departed later to begin a honeymoon on Nantucket."

Ellsworth Grant recalled: The Hepburn family celebrated holidays in style, especially Thanksgiving and Christmas. In the early years of our marriage, Marion and I took part in the Christmas day festivities, which—to be honest—were a madhouse. A large Christmas tree was set up in the living room; the floor around littered with presents. The hi-fi player installed by Luddy, Katharine's ex-husband, blared away. Dr. and Mrs. Hepburn danced a jig. Luddy was everywhere with his movie camera. We began the ordeal by lining up at the top of the stairs according to height, not age, and marching down singing some carol.

Then, the opening of the gifts would begin. Katharine sat on the floor, handing them out, one by one, for Bob and Suzy, Peg and Tom, Marion and myself, Dick and Betty, Phyllis Wilbourn, and Luddy, and some tagged for the small children. As fast as the wrappings were torn apart, Dr. Hepburn would gather up all the paper and rush

Circa 1932

outdoors to dump it all into the incinerator at the rear of the garden. This ritual caused consternation, because he took the tags too and in a few instances envelopes with checks and cash. By the time dinner was served by faithful Fanny, the family housekeeper and former nurse, we were all quite exhausted.

After the war, Hepburn's sister Peg Perry and her husband Tom bought a farm on Barbourtown Road in the center of Canton, Connecticut. The old house of locally quarried stone had been built in 1843. The Perrys raised sheep and, later, cattle. Peg started a big vegetable garden. The family was amazed how thoroughly Peg had adapted to rural living. She and Tom raised five children—twins Tommy and Nomi and three sons, Robert, Scott, and Lance. Peg, who had as much energy as her sister Katharine, became the Canton librarian. She also enjoyed hosting Thanksgiving. Every year she rose at four o'clock to put a twenty-pound turkey in the oven, bake delicious rolls, prepare all the fixings, and set the tables, adults in the dining room, children in the living room.

Around noon, the guests began to arrive. The cousins would noisily cavort around. There would be a roaring fire in the large stone fireplace. On a coffee table were sherry and cider, cheese, celery, and olives. Before dinner, there was a usually a touch football game on the south lawn.

At last, like a whirlwind, came Katharine and Phyllis, carrying flowers and candies. At dinner, Tom carved the turkey as skillfully as he butchered a sheep. For dessert there were pies (apple, pumpkin, and squash) and plenty of vanilla ice cream. Afterward, whatever the weather, the tribe would set out on a long walk along Barbourtown Road to inspect Tom's factory and climb the watchtower he built for a view of the western hills and New Hartford.

Stuffed with food, I can tell you, I was a tired father and glad to get home by six o'clock.

Ellsworth Grant recalled: With the making of *On Golden Pond* with co-star Henry Fonda in 1981, Katharine had reached the peak of her long career. She was now seventy-two years old and the only female star of her generation still working. *On Golden Pond,* her forty-fifth feature film, won her a fourth Oscar.

At this point in her life, she was spending more time at Fenwick, even in winter. On Monday morning, December 14, 1982, Katharine was driving into Old Saybrook with seventy-three-year-old Phyllis Wilbourn, her longtime companion and secretary, probably headed to Walt's for groceries or to Patrick's Country Store for clothing. The causeway from Fenwick to Saybrook Point was slippery, and when Katharine reached for something on the front seat, she lost control of the car and smashed into a utility pole.

Katharine knew right away they were both seriously injured, she had caught her foot under the accelerator and Phyllis was semi-conscious. When the police came, she yelled, "Take us by ambulance to Hartford Hospital."

Phyllis sustained a fractured left wrist, two cracked ribs, and a minor spinal injury. Katharine nearly severed her right ankle. Her injury was far more serious than reported to the press, and it would be a long convalescence. Where did they go to recover? Neither to Fenwick nor to New York; they went to her sister's house.

On New Year's Day an ambulance rolled into the driveway of our house on Steele Road in West Hartford. Kate was in a cast up to her hip. I had never seen her look so pale and frail. Our bedroom had been converted into a hospital suite with around-the-clock medical

The Philadelphia Story (Shubert Theater, 1939)

care. Marion and I moved to the third-floor bedroom. The house was so full of floral arrangements that it looked like the Garden of Eden!

Kate's vitality soon reasserted itself; you just couldn't stop her from running the show. I had to install a special phone to handle her constant calls. A repairman who came to fix my typewriter in the third-floor office spotted Katharine in her bed and yelped, 'Good God!'

Katharine answered, "Don't be surprised, come in and sit down."

By the end of February she was mobile. Dr. Pasternak wanted her to strengthen her ankle by swimming. It so happened I had friends with an indoor pool only two blocks away, and every morning she swam there. She walked through Elizabeth Park, surprising gardeners in the greenhouse; visited the Mark Twain House, the Noah Webster House, and the Hillstead Museum in Farmington. I also drove her around town to see all of her old haunts, including 201 Bloomfield Avenue (then occupied by the University of Hartford), the West Middle School she attended, and the West Hartford reservoirs she loved to walk around. The entire episode, which might be called "Guess Who's Coming to Get Well," was, as Marion said, "a happy and healing experience for us all."

I drove to Fenwick on a very rainy summer day. The wind was howling as I came across the causeway that connects Old Saybrook to Fenwick. White caps were rolling high in the sea, but I didn't mind; I was excited to meet Schuyler Grant, great niece of Katharine Hepburn! Grant lives just down the way from the Hepburn mansion in a home she inherited from her grandmother, Hepburn's sister, Marion Hepburn Grant, and was in Fenwick for an end-of-summer stay with her family. We chatted for a long time, sitting in a large, cozy window seat as it stormed outside her rambling home.

Now in her forties, Grant remembers when she was ten or twelve years old thinking she might be able to become President of the United States, as a democrat, of course. She explained that when you have someone as famous as Hepburn in your family, it didn't seem unreasonable that you could be famous too. But by her early twenties she abandoned the idea of being the commander-in-chief, and Katharine Hepburn was just her "Aunt Kat."

But things were not always rosy between Grant and her aunt. Grant recalled her "best" acting story about Hepburn. When Grant was a preteen, Hepburn, by now on in years but always the teacher who gave her niece zero slack, was approached by a Canadian production company to play the part of Marilla in *Anne of Green Gables*. In a dead-on Hepburn trans-Atlantic voice, Grant relays her aunt's response to the production company: "I will never play the second lead. I will only be the star, so . . . I can play Anne."

The producers weren't sold on the idea and told Hepburn she was way too old for the part, to which the star replied that she would not be involved with the production at all, but perhaps her twelve-year-old niece Schuyler, who at the time was living in northern California, could play Anne.

Grant says the producers thought if they cast her, then maybe they could persuade Hepburn to play Marilla and get the press they were looking for. Knowing her aunt's strong will, Grant knew that was never going to happen, that Hepburn would never play the second lead, ever, in her lifetime. She says Hepburn would have preferred to play the lead in a bad made-for-television-movie-of-the-week than play second fiddle in a film. She set the bar very high for herself, always.

> "LIFE IS HARD, AFTER ALL, IT KILLS YOU."
> —katharine hepburn

That summer in Fenwick, Hepburn decided she would coach Grant on how to be an actress. She spent her summers in the borough with her grandmother and was expected to report to her aunt's home for acting lessons every day. Hepburn would coach her on her lines.

"It was a nightmare," remembers Grant, explaining that she and Hepburn didn't exactly see eye to eye. Grant was living in a modern, post-actor's studio world, unlike what Hepburn had known. She thought people should just be natural, not stiff as were the actors in her aunt's era. Hepburn wanted her to speak in a trans-Atlantic or mid-Atlantic voice, as was taught to actors and actresses in the 1930s, '40s, and early '50s.

The "put on" voice of that time, the way in which Hepburn spoke in her films, was common then. It was a rather fast-talking, fake accent with an emphasis on t's and dropped r sounds. It was an attempt to mimic a kind of aristocracy, someone who spent her time between America and Britain, a hybrid of the two countries. The accent was taught in some schools of high society. It is written that Katharine Hepburn and Cary Grant, both A-list movie stars, crafted this accent the best in Hollywood. It eventually went away after World War II or so, when the public embraced people just being themselves.

Schuyler said that Hepburn spoke with that accent always, even at home. That was her persona. It wasn't quite as "mannered" or as "stagy" around family, but it was constant. So when Hepburn tried to get Anne of Green Gables to sound like she thought an actress should, it was "a twelve-year-old's worst nightmare." Hepburn had Grant sit in a chair at her home and would spoon-feed her as to how she should say her lines.

Grant, like her aunt, was pretty stubborn and would argue and say, "No, nobody talks like this anymore." She told Hepburn it wasn't natural that a child would never speak like that in a film. Things would usually go downhill from there. Hepburn would lash back and say that anybody else would give their right pinkie finger to get acting lessons from Katharine Hepburn, to which Grant barked back, "I don't care, you don't know anything about acting these days." This back and forth would go on all summer long in Fenwick, huge verbal fights ending with Hepburn telling her niece to, "Go away and don't come back."

That stalemate would last about a week and then Hepburn would send word that Grant was invited back for another acting lesson, to which Grant would think *No way.* It was so painful for the both of them and so "completely dysfunctional." The two of them finally agreed to end the acting lessons and try and salvage what was left of the summer in peace.

After all of that, Grant did not even get the lead in the movie. She was asked to play a different part to which her aunt told her, "Don't do it! If you take the second lead now, you'll never be a star."

While doubtful at the time, Grant admits now that Hepburn was right. She never ended up being a star, but she did accept the part and had a lot of fun doing it.

Hepburn had, in her niece's words, "Singularity of mind and purpose." In her later years, she was cast in a series of mediocre television films of the week, and starred in all of them, turning down second lead parts in other films.

Ellsworth Grant recalled: The first time I saw Katharine Hepburn was in 1934. I was seventeen years old, a callow youth mesmerized by this vision with shoulder-length reddish hair, willowy figure, and commanding manner. She was standing on a ladder and decorating the living room of her parents' house on Bloomfield Avenue in West Hartford for a dance during Christmas vacation for her younger sisters, Marion and Peg.

Katharine was already a new star in Hollywood with six or seven features to her credit, including *Morning Glory* and the award-winning *Little Women.* To the surprise of staid, old, "waspish" Hartfordites, some of whose hierarchy had always viewed the Hepburns as non-conformist, one of their own had brought fame overnight to their town.

When Katharine played Bushnell Memorial Hall in Hartford, she acknowledged where she came from. Back stage visiting artists had a tradition of autographing a wall. Katharine scribbled her name and below it wrote, "Hometown girl."

"Why aren't you coming to our dance this year?" she demanded as she descended the ladder.

I stammered, feeling as though I was betraying my tenuous relations with Marion's family, trying to explain I had been invited to a house party in Bloomfield Hills, Michigan.

"Too bad," she murmured.

On the U.S. tour of *Jane Eyre* (1936–1937)

I had first met Marion at a similar dance the previous year. The boys came from Kingswood School, the girls from Oxford School in West Hartford (the two elite schools merged in 1969). Marion, I soon discovered, was a special kind of girl, flirtatious and smart. Her gruff father scared me, but I quickly fell in with her mother.

Katharine came home at every opportunity, where she was treated as just another member of the family. Her former husband, Ludlow "Luddy" Ogden Smith, frequently accompanied her. He loved to take movies of arduous Sunday outings—golfing, skating, walking in the woods. In the spring there was a contest to see who would be first to find a jack-in-the-pulpit. Katharine always won. Other guests I remember were producer Leland Hayward, director George Stevens, and Katharine's good friend Laura Harding."

Ellsworth Grant was married to Katharine Hepburn's sister Marion. He was a prolific writer, documentary filmmaker, Connecticut historian, and former mayor of West Hartford. He had a ringside seat to most of the legendary actress's very long life. He met her when he was dating Marion; Hepburn had just won her first Academy Award.

"Hartford," recalled Katharine Hepburn, "is where I learned of life's adventure. I was freckled and wore my hair like a boy's. With one older brother, Tom, and two younger, Dick and Bob, being a girl was a torment. I used to climb the hemlock tree in our front yard and sit for hours on the top. People would pass, call Dad and Mother, and say, "Kathy is up on the top of that tree." Mother would answer, "Yes, don't alarm her, she might fall off."

"One of my crimes was to run up a charge account at Child's Drug Store for Hershey bars and licorice sticks. As my capacity was infinite, this finally had to be stopped. I can eat a pound of chocolates with joy. Training is important.

"Back then, everyone called me Kathy. They might as well have called me Tom. I was a tomboy. I could out dive, out swim, out run, out climb anybody. I could stand on my hands and hang upside down by my toes from a trapeze 30 feet above our gravel driveway.

"I am, totally, completely, the product of two fascinating individuals who happened to be my parents. They gave me the values and the sense of self worth and drive that I needed. Life at our house was always surprising; we entertained famous people. Mother and Dad argued only about politics. At the dinner table every conceivable topic was discussed—venereal disease, feminism, Marxism, Darwinism, and even crime."

—as told to Ellsworth Grant

Over the fireplace of Hepburn's childhood home hung the inscription "Listen to the Song of Life." It became the revered symbol for the active family of three boys and three girls, as well as their parents.

"HARTFORD IS WHERE I FIRST LEARNED ABOUT THE IMPORTANCE OF BEING SURE I DID THE BEST I COULD DO. I HAVE TRAVELED THE WORLD FROM HARTFORD IN PURSUIT OF VITALITY AND OF FULFILLING WORK, BUT WHEN I LOOK AROUND, I KNOW WHAT I REALLY NEED IS RIGHT HERE IN MY HOMETOWN."

—katharine hepburn

Circa 1940s

katharine the star

In the summer of 1939, Ellsworth Grant was job hunting in New York and stayed at Katharine's four-story brownstone at 244 49th Street. *The Philadelphia Story* had reached Broadway, and around five p.m., before each performance, Katharine would dine on steak and ice cream. It surprised me to hear her admit that just before the curtain rose she felt so nervous she sometimes threw up. Afterward there would be a late supper. Once she challenged me to play chess with Luddy and offered $10.00 to the winner. I lost.

One day she asked me to attend a cocktail party in the apartment of Nancy Davis on her behalf. Davis was then an aspiring actress who was the adopted daughter of Dr. Loyal Davis, a prominent Chicago surgeon. Besides being pretty and ambitious, Davis didn't impress me as exceptional, and certainly not destined to become First Lady, which of course she did.

Life at 244 was frenetic. The telephone and doorbell rang constantly. There seemed to be a

May   Wal
DBSON · CATL

steady round of little dramas over the furnace, the smoking fireplace, the leaking roof, or the security system. The ménage consisted of Emily Perkins, the cook; Wei Fung who spoke only Chinese; and Charles, who was the handyman, bodyguard, and chauffeur. An ex-pugilist, Charles was the unofficial mayor of 49th Street. Short and stocky, his gray hair crew cut, he saw to it that the police never tagged Miss Hepburn's Lincoln at the curb. Whenever we visited New York, invariably Charles would be painting walls like mad. He painted the inside so many times, the house seemed to grow smaller year by year.

Ellsworth Grant recalled: Katharine Hepburn's Fenwick bedroom faced Long Island Sound to the south and the mouth of the Connecticut River to the east, with its inner and outer lighthouses. She often painted the scene in watercolors. She also liked to go out with her brother Dick in his canoe around the outer lighthouse, across the river, and into the Lyme marshes, but she was also well aware that the river had a reputation for being polluted. When making the film *Summertime* in Venice in 1955, she was required to fall over backward into the Grand Canal for a particular scene. Director David Mclean refused to let her do it.

"It's too polluted," he said. "We'll use your understudy."

"You forget, David," she replied. "I was brought up on the Connecticut River."

Hepburn did the scene herself.

Filming *Summertime* in Venice (1955)

Ellsworth Grant recalled: For more than sixty years, the Connecticut River had so high a coliform bacteria count that it was unsuitable for any kind of recreational use. I had been boating on the river ever since I was a teenager, so I inspired to make a film about its historical significance as a highway of trade and its importance as a natural resource.

I told Katharine about the project one day and she asked, "Who's going to narrate it?" I told her I had an announcer from WTIC-TV in Connecticut in mind. He was also helping me with the editing.

"No, I think I can do it better," she replied.

Thrilled, I sent her the script and she recorded it. The result was a half-hour documentary called *The Long Tidal River*, completed in 1965. It was an instant success. It was shown all around the state, Katharine's description of the river as "a beautifully landscaped cesspool" roused the public's outrage. The governor appointed a 100-man task force to develop an action program, of which I became vice-chairman.

Intrigued about the film's popularity, Katharine asked me to send her a print, which she projected one evening to Spencer Tracy. His only comment? "You talk too much!"

It was true, there *was* too much narration for a half-hour film, but somehow it worked. The legislation unanimously adopted a $150 million dollar bonding program, and within fifteen years, nearly half of the river and its tributaries had been restored for recreational use. From Middletown to the mouth of the river it was once again swimmable.

Ellsworth Grant recalled: It was an exciting, memorable night with a near disastrous ending. In February 1971, Katharine Hepburn came back to Hartford with her musical *Coco,* based on the life of the famous French fashion designer Coco Chanel. It was Hepburn's second stage appearance at the Bushnell Theater, her first had been in 1942 when she starred in *Without Love.*

The opening performance was a benefit for the Urban League of Hartford, which her sister Marion helped found. The enthusiastic full house clapped when Katharine first appeared and clapped many more times before the end. When the final curtain came down, she was given a standing ovation, and then she spoke for a few minutes about how it felt to play her hometown again: "It's a very emotional and extraordinary experience. With my brothers and sisters and my relatives, my nephews and nieces in the audience. It an experience I can't describe."

After the performance, some 300 members of the Urban League and their friends flocked to the Colonial Room to meet Katharine and the cast. It must have been one o'clock in the morning before the family returned to 201 Bloomfield Avenue—Kate; her secretary, Phyllis Wilbourn; her brother Bob, a surgeon at the Hartford Hospital; his wife, Susannah; Marion; and myself. Kate was nervous. She told us that at the last venue she had to fire her chauffeur. She was afraid, because the woman was so distraught, that she might have followed the musical to Hartford. It turned out the woman was extremely jealous of Phyllis and wanted her job.

Mark Hellinger Theatre

PLAYBILL

the national magazine for theatregoers

COCO

At 201, the lights were on. Rushing in, Kate said she would check the rooms. We waited in the kitchen. A few minutes later there were screams upstairs, and the ex-chauffeur came running down to the kitchen pursued by her ex-employer. They collided in the doorway to the garage, Kate on top, struggling to push her out. Kate swore and yelled, "She's bit my finger!" The woman fled.

It was a nasty bite, right to the bone. Bob phoned an orthopedic specialist and rushed Kate to Hartford Hospital. I called the police, who eventually caught the woman. There was nothing more we could do that night, and we feared the show would have to close. But we underestimated Kate's fortitude in the face of adversity. In a classic example of "the show must go on" tradition, she appeared at her matinee the next day—her hand and arm bandaged and held high.

Signed Playbill from *Coco* (1969–1970)

Ellsworth Grant recalled: In 1976, we put an addition on my house in Old Saybrook, Connecticut, that included a projection room. For some years I had been collecting 16 mm prints of Katharine's films, some of which she had never viewed. So, accompanied by Phyllis Wilbourn, her secretary, she would sit on the floor, watch her films, and critique her work. While I didn't record all her observations, here are some comments I remember:

On *Bill of Divorcement*, her first movie made in 1932, she said, "I learned a tremendous lot from John Barrymore. Raves!"

In 1935 she made *Alice Adams* for which she was nominated for an Academy Award. She gave it a "raves," but thought it was "very much neglected by the film historians."

She thought *Sylvia Scarlett* was "a total disaster!"

She wrapped *Break of Hearts* up by calling it a "bore."

Of *Mary of Scotland* she just said, "Roasted." Perhaps she meant the costumes were hot.

She thought both *A Woman Rebels* and *Quality Street* were "poor."

To her 1937 *Stage Door* she gave that one word, "Raves."

In 1938 she made her first comedy, *Bringing Up Baby,* to which she said, "Very funny; didn't do well. Now a classic."

By then, 1938, Katharine had become "poison" in Hollywood. Her career was in shambles. She moaned about how she couldn't get a job. Then she was saved and elevated to new stardom by the play *Philadelphia Story* in 1939 and the film in 1940. With *Woman of the*

Katharine on the set of *Bringing Up Baby* (1938)

Year in 1942, her first film with Spencer Tracy, she continued to excel. She went on to make nine features with Tracy. In all she won four best actress Oscars.

As I recall, she had never seen *The African Queen* before, and I know she wouldn't look at her films with Tracy or her last feature *On Golden Pond.* They were just too personal.

What are the odds that I would someday own and wear a coat once belonging to Katharine Hepburn? I mean really, a kid from South Bend, Indiana? As it turns out, those odds are pretty good. Being a reporter in television can do that for you, you just never know where you will go, who you will meet, or what fundraising event you might be asked to emcee, which was the case that united me with the coat.

It was a Planned Parenthood event, the kind of organization Hepburn held dear. She was all about women's rights, a passion passed down to her by her social activist mother, Katharine Martha Houghton Hepburn. Her mother had been instrumental in helping

women earn the right to vote. She also helped form the Connecticut Birth Control League in 1923. Hepburn had worked right alongside her mother to see that women were no longer considered second-class citizens.

This particular event was a fundraiser for Planned Parenthood of Southern New England, Inc. Hepburn's niece, Katharine Houghton Grant, was the guest of honor. Grant was the recipient of many of Hepburn's belongings and gave some items, including the Valentina red wool coat, to the organization to be auctioned off. So it came to be that on October 27, 2011, I tried that coat on. It fit like a glove. I won the bid and now that beautiful

The author's Valentina red coat previously owned by Kate.

garment hangs right there in my closet! I wear it every winter with a little smile on my face knowing it was part of Hepburn's personal collection.

> "THE WOMAN'S POSITION IN THE WORLD TODAY IS SO MUCH HARDER THAN A MAN'S THAT IT MAKES ME CHOKE EVERY TIME I HEAR A MAN COMPLAIN ABOUT ANYTHING."
>
> —katharine hepburn

The history behind this coat is wonderful. It was designed by Valentina Nicholaevna Sanina Schlee, who was born in Kiev, Ukraine, in 1899. Valentina was a designer for the biggest Hollywood stars in the 1930s, '40s, and '50s. Her clients aside from Hepburn included Greta Garbo and Gloria Swanson. Valentina, a style icon herself, designed for movies and stage and did the costuming for Hepburn for the 1939 stage version of *The Philadelphia Story* as well as many of her movies.

Valentina was known for creating long, flowing, simple gowns and was sought after in Hollywood by stars who could wear that look well, which Hepburn could. Judy Samelson, former editor of Playbill and what I would call an authority on Hepburn, wrote that Hepburn called Valentina "genius" and latched onto her, knowing she would keep her looking like a star.

Kent State University Museum in Ohio is the keeper of many of Hepburn's costumes from stage and the movies. According to the museum's website, the costumes were acquired in 2008 and were collected right out of Hepburn's closet following her death as stipulated by Hepburn herself, who before she died in 2003, made it clear that her collection of performance clothes should be given to an educational institution instead of being sold at auction. Kent State was chosen as the recipient because it is internationally known for its costumes and fashion collections. Occasionally, the collection tours the country, as it did in 2015, making a stop at the historical society in Hartford.

Actor Sam Waterston, who co-starred with Katharine Hepburn in the 1973 television film *The Glass Menagerie*, remembers Hepburn coming to him one day in the middle of shooting and told him, "Your clock's not ticking, and when your clock's not ticking you're awfully dull!" She then went on, saying, "But when your clock is ticking you're, very, very interesting . . . SO START YOUR CLOCK!"

Not sure how to respond, he dutifully replied, "Yes, Ma'am!"

British film director Anthony Harvey says his relationship with Katharine Hepburn was a series of disagreements and fights. He says she loved to put him in his place whenever possible, but he loved working with her all the same and they stayed friends forever. Initially he says his meetings with her went "very badly." He wasn't sure if they were going to "get on" at all, ever.

One such occasion was when Harvey presented Hepburn with an opportunity to star in his 1966 British drama *The Dutchman,* which he thought was "pretty damn good." Peter O'Toole was slated to be in the film and Harvey agreed to take it to Hollywood to present it to Hepburn.

However, Hepburn, who was already working with O'Toole on another Harvey film, *Lion in the Winter*, wasn't exactly welcoming. Harvey wasn't sure his film with her would ever be made because she was so difficult. Well, the picture did get made, and in grand fashion. Hepburn won an Oscar for her performance, tying with Barbra

The Glass Menagerie (1973)

Streisand for her role in *Funny Girl*, and Harvey was nominated for an Academy Award.

> "LIFE IS TO BE LIVED. IF YOU HAVE TO SUPPORT YOURSELF, YOU HAD BLOODY WELL BETTER FIND SOME WAY THAT IS GOING TO BE INTERESTING. AND YOU DON'T DO THAT BY SITTING AROUND."
>
> —katharine hepburn

Looking back, Harvey remembers a directing moment in which he told Hepburn that she should show real vulnerability, that she should "let down her hair."

"I don't do that," Hepburn told him.

To which he replied, "Well, then, I'm not shooting the scene." The stalemate was on.

Hepburn then shot back, "Oh really!"

Harvey says he had had it with her and they had a "bloody great row." Hepburn finally said she would compromise, but Harvey was having none of it. He said she finally played the scene his way and it was stunning. That night, he remembers, he found a tissue on the floor that had been pushed under the door of his hotel room. On it these words: "Dear Tony, I hope the stars, the sun, and the moon are with you. C'mon and have dinner." It was signed, "Kate." That began their real friendship.

Harvey also recounts a time he went to Hepburn's place in Fenwick. He was there in the wintertime and there was thick ice near the shore of her home. He saw her break the ice so she could get in and swim. He laughed at her and thought it was just crazy what she was doing. He remembers saying, "God, Kate, this is something else."

"Well, you know I do this to annoy my guests," she replied, then admitted to him that she didn't enjoy swimming in the cold water at all. He laughs as he recalls this time in his life with her and what a character she was.

Everett Raymond Kinstler is a famed portrait artist who was commissioned to depict many movie stars and seven US presidents. His paintings of Presidents Ford and Reagan are the official White House portraits. Kinstler did many works of Hepburn in oil and other mediums, including the one that hangs in the Smithsonian National Portrait Gallery Permanent Collection, near her four best actress Oscars.

Kinstler remembers one meeting he had with the actress in the summer of 1981. She was rehearsing the play *The West Side Waltz* in New York City with Dorothy Loudon at the Barrymore Theatre. He

Portrait © Everett Raymond Kinstler

wanted to talk to her about a project he was working on to preserve the library at The Players' Club, a private social club in New York whose members are from the international theatre community and the fields of film, television, music, and publishing as well as patrons of the arts. He wasn't sure how Hepburn would react to his request, because for much of its history, The Players Club was only open to men. It wasn't until 1989 that the first woman, actress Helen Hayes, was admitted.

Kinstler called Hepburn from Gramercy Park, which was about 20 blocks from where she lived in the city at the time. She told him she didn't know where Gramercy Park was, which of course was a lie; she knew quite well where it was. She told him to come to her place straight away. He complied, stopping for flowers first because this was, after all, Katharine Hepburn.

He arrived and they had dinner together. They discussed Kinstler doing a portrait of Hepburn in order to raise money for the library. He

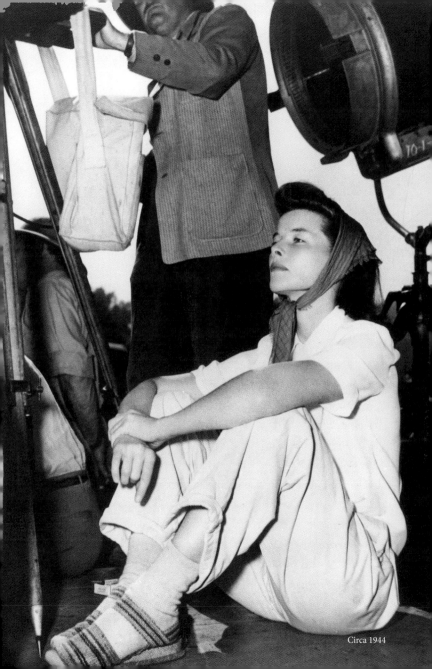

Circa 1944

remembers sitting with Hepburn when her niece, Katharine Houghton, came down the stairs. Hepburn introduced her to Kinstler and explained to her that he wanted to do a painting of her for The Players Club.

"Isn't that the all-male actors club in Gramercy Park?" Houghton asked.

Kinstler thought this was going to be the deal breaker. Hepburn would hardly like the fact that it was men only.

"Katharine, we're doing this to save the library at The Player's Club," Hepburn said briskly. "Spencer was a member."

Bang, that was the end of the discussion, Kinstler said. If Spencer Tracy was involved, Hepburn would have no problem with the old boys' club to help raise money for its library with her likeness.

Katharine Hepburn graced the stage of the Shakespeare Festival Theater in Stratford for two summers as part of the American Shakespeare Festival. In 1957, Hepburn played the role of Portia in the *Merchant of Venice* and Beatrice in *Much Ado About Nothing*. In 1960 she played Viola in *Twelfth Night* and Cleopatra in *Anthony and Cleopatra*. Her iconic status brought in the crowds, as well as other megawatt stage stars, some of who were young upstarts who ended up becoming famous in their own rights.

Though the theater has been closed for decades, one can see how it was a draw in the day. It was located on the water in the shoreline town with beautiful grounds around it. The theater's memorabilia is now stacked in boxes in a nearby historic home in which the actors rehearsed. There are photos and an original costume or two of Hepburn's along with letters and telegrams from her.

Chris Rooney is part of a group of folks who feel strongly about reviving the theater one day. Proud of the artifacts they have saved, she expanded on how important Hepburn was to the venue in its early days. "In terms of the theater, she was a magnet for its success. In the years she was here, that she was performing, she enabled the theater to not only draw

One of Kate's costumes from the Shakespeare Festival Theater in Stratford, Connecticut.

audiences, but to draw other talent. That was the absolute pinnacle of talent in the country."

Rooney went on to say that because of Hepburn's involvement, the theater attracted "bit" actors who went on to become famous. For instance both Christopher Walken and a young Ed Asner came. According to Rooney, Asner "got a call to do a small part right after he got married in 1957 and in those days, if you got a call to this theater you came on your knees, it was such an honor to be here."

"Kate was the magnet who drew all the talent, who drew all the audiences that made it a success," he said. "Once she stopped performing at the theater, it went downhill."

While Hepburn was performing at the Shakespeare Festival Theater in Stratford, she was accused of taking lettuce and other vegetables from what was commonly known as Will Gere's Herb Garden, or the Shakespeare Garden. Gere performed in many plays at the theater, later he would be most known for the role of Grandpa Zebulon Tyler Walton on the 1970s television series, *The Waltons.*

As the story goes, when Spencer Tracy would come into town to stay at Hepburn's cottage near the theater on the water, she would wander up the street and pilfer things out of Will's garden. One day she and Gere had a confrontation right there among the plants. Hepburn took a $20 bill out of her pocket and threw it at Gere, saying, "Here you go, you old crank. Here's twenty bucks for your lettuce."

Gere indeed took her money. He bought a small tree with it and planted it near the theater museum building on the property. It's in honor of Ms. Hepburn. It is a flowering crab.

According to Chris Rooney, when Katharine Hepburn was in residence at the Shakespeare Festival Theater, she declined a nice, big, white home offered to her on the waterfront of the Housatonic River. Instead she opted for an old shack of a cottage that was "in" the river, up on stilts. When you think about it, except for its size, it was kind of the same set up the star had in Fenwick . . . water on the front that made it more private for her. Nobody could see into the front of it unless you were in a small boat or canoe.

Antony and Cleopatra (1960) at the Shakespeare Festival Theater with Robert Ryan.

Hepburn's secretary lived in the big white house for the time that Hepburn was on stage in Stratford. Chris told me that "Kate kept her little boat in a shack on the grounds of the big house. She would pull the boat out often. She was quite athletic."

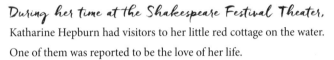

During her time at the Shakespeare Festival Theater, Katharine Hepburn had visitors to her little red cottage on the water. One of them was reported to be the love of her life.

"People would say they saw Spencer Tracy walking from the train station in Stratford," remembers Chris Rooney. "He and Hepburn would spend time outside on the porch of the little red house, chatting. There was a raised walkway to get out to the little red cottage, which is how the actress and anybody else was able to access it."

Someone who knew that Spencer or "Spence" came to call a lot was Millie Patria. Millie was married to Joe Patria, who worked on all the staging at the Shakespeare Festival Theater. She and Joe became good friends with Hepburn and other stars. They didn't treat her or anybody else as any big deal, they knew they were famous, but they also knew they were wonderful, intelligent people who were fun to be around. Millie had many a chat with Hepburn, sometimes over tea looking out over the water at her cottage. Joe used to take Hepburn and Tracy fishing when there was some downtime. When they wanted to get away, he would just take them out and spend time with them, just like friends do.

Millie Patria whose husband worked on all the staging at the Shakespeare Festival Theater has fond memories of her time spent with Katharine Hepburn. She was pregnant with her first son, Michael, when the friendship first started. Millie says at that time Hepburn was about her mother's age. She remembers that her mom and Hepburn were both born in 1907, which would have put the star in her mid-fifties at the time.

Hepburn would send word for Millie to come down and visit her at the little red cottage and they would chat. Millie loved seeing her and would look forward to walking onto the ramp off the tiny road that lead to the cottage. The view from the porch was so peaceful, nothing but water and nature, so private. She never saw Hepburn take a swim while she was in Stratford, but she knows she did, just like at her home in Fenwick, no matter the weather.

Millie says the two of them were close because Hepburn knew that Millie saw her as just a person, not a megawatt movie star, none of that was in the way and they could just talk. Millie says Hepburn enjoyed showing Millie all of her watercolor paintings that hung on one wall in her place. It relaxed Hepburn when she painted, said Millie. Always the perfectionist, Hepburn sought Millie's advice about her work as an artist, she wanted her opinions. Millie had studied art in college at the University of Bridgeport.

"I was very, very frank with her," Millie said. "I pointed out what I thought were not the greatest. I told her about some of the mistakes I thought she was making. She greatly appreciated my candidness, she appreciated that, and was very grateful. I was being truly honest with her. I wasn't big-eyed about her being such a special person, that just wasn't my make up to go crazy over movie stars."

"We would sit and have tea," Millie remembered. "I would go into the little bathroom there, and it was something. Spencer Tracy's pictures were all over the walls and she had this little round table that had cologne on it and powder. I think the name of the cologne was 4711."

"In Hepburn's bedroom there were tons of books," Millie says. "She had a tufted backrest on her bed so she could lie there and read."

"LET'S JUST SAY THAT WHERE A CHANGE WAS REQUIRED, I ADJUSTED. IN EVERY RELATIONSHIP THAT EXISTS, PEOPLE HAVE TO SEEK A WAY TO SURVIVE. IF YOU REALLY CARE ABOUT THE PERSON, YOU DO WHAT'S NECESSARY, OR THAT'S THE END. FOR THE FIRST TIME, I FOUND THAT I REALLY COULD CHANGE, AND THE QUALITIES I MOST ADMIRED IN MYSELF I GAVE UP. I STOPPED BEING LOUD AND BOSSY... OH, ALL RIGHT. I WAS STILL LOUD AND BOSSY, BUT ONLY BEHIND HIS BACK."

—katharine hepburn

Millie goes on to say that Spencer Tracy came to call a lot, and he stayed at the cottage with Hepburn. Mille says she "bumped into Tracy before she was even introduced to him inside the Shakespeare Festival Theater. She was just walking around and happened to open a door and slammed right into him. Of that first glance she says, "He was quite something, I mean I was quite young at the time, probably about twenty-five, but I thought, *Wow, what a good looking guy.*"

Millie says Hepburn was lovely and sweet to her and "really a wonderful person and very, very, very, intelligent. We had wonderful conversations." Millie also told me that Hepburn gladly picnicked with all the folks who worked at the theater from time to time.

While there were many photos taken of her and Hepburn, Millie does not have even one of them and that makes her sad. But she does have one gift from the actress.

At the end of the theater season, Millie's husband told her that "Katie" had left her something. "It was all wrapped in white tissue paper with pink ribbons. It was one of her paintings of the Shakespeare Festival Theater and she inscribed it to "Joe." She used to call me "Mrs. Joe. I cherish that gift."

Millie told me she wished she had kept a journal about her chats with Hepburn and about all the famous people she met over the years with her husband as he went on to style sets for most of the world's famous plays on Broadway in the US and then in Europe. Alas, she did not write anything down about her glimpses into the lives of the famous. She says it is a shame because what stories she could then remember to tell.

Joe Patria was one of the most famous stage carpenters in the area. He and others like him work to make sure the infrastructures of the stage work hand in hand with the scenery. The "loading in" of the show is extremely important. Guys like Patria understand when theater seats need to be moved, the relationships between walls and flooring, and everything that makes up the feel of a show. They make sure all parts work together. In the end they make sure the illusion of theater works for those coming to see a show.

Originally attending the University of Bridgeport on the GI Bill after serving as a marine, Patria gave up his studies to be a teacher when he found his calling at the Shakespeare Festival Theater. He dropped out of college and moved up the ranks quickly. Even though he was one of the youngest carpenters on the payroll, he was soon in charge of the back stage for the prominent 1,500-seat venue.

Eventually, he moved on to do Broadway shows, where his job is to take the blueprints from the set designer, go to the shops, and tell them how he wants everything made. Then he leads the way for the "load ins" of the shows. He is a technical coordinator of the highest note, having done hundreds of shows, including *Phantom, Les Miserables, Miss Saigon,* and *Annie.*

According to his wife, Millie, Patria connected with Hepburn as well as she did. She remembers one day when he yawned on the stage. He was tired, often working twelve or fourteen hours a day. Hepburn saw him yawning, and called him over. She told him to go over to the little house she was renting while she was there and go into the bedroom, lie down, and take a nap. Hepburn also told him that under

Holiday (1938)

the sink he would see a bottle of Four Roses bourbon. She told him, "Have a little shot and go take a little nap."

"Hepburn was just fun and kind and incredible, she really was," said Millie Patria. "She was one of the brightest people I've ever met." Millie remembers that from time to time her husband, Joe, would go over to the little house that Hepburn was renting while working at the Shakespeare Festival Theater in Stratford, Connecticut, and have some drinks with Spencer Tracy. They would just sit on the tiny front porch of the tiny red house and look out over the water, said Millie. It was an amazing moment in time between a guy who built stages and a megawatt Academy Award–winning Hollywood super star. "But I expect," said Millie, "at that time they were just two guys on a porch."

Kay Hall, a volunteer at the Katharine Hepburn Cultural Arts Center (The Kate) in Old Saybrook remembers a story about a buyer interested in the Old Saybrook printing company for which Hall worked running into Katharine Hepburn while she was playing Coco Chanel in *Coco.* This buyer was staying in the same hotel with Hepburn and ended up sitting next to the star in the bar one night. He was having a nightcap with another patron who also happened to be from Old Saybrook. They wanted to strike up a conversation with Hepburn, but decided not to bother her. As it happens Hepburn overheard her town's name and struck up a conversation with *them.*

The next day, as the story goes, there was a little incident with Hepburn and an overzealous fan who would not leave her alone. Kay tells me the buyer and Hepburn were standing outside. Hepburn was waiting for her car when this guy came running up to her and insisted on taking her photo. Hepburn started screaming at him with some "interesting language," nearly punching him, and that's when the doorman from the hotel got involved and tried to put an end to the ugly scene. He told Hepburn to go back into the hotel and that he would take care of things. No sooner had this unruly tourist been banished, and Hepburn given the all clear, he was back again and on Hepburn. Hepburn knocked the camera out of his hand and drop kicked it into the street.

Hall said it was known throughout town that you never approached Kate. Like royalty in the UK, you waited for *her* to talk to *you.*

In the 1970s, the Bombaci family planted a one-acre, pick-your-own blueberry field on Bokum Road in Essex, Connecticut. Mark Bombaci was in high school when their most famous customer found their farm. Little did they know it would become a favorite of Katharine Hepburn's. She would venture to the farm, mostly on weekends. Sometimes she would come by herself, other times she brought along family members or colleagues. Mark remembers seeing Hollywood greats such as movie director Anthony Harvey and the daughter of famous American film producer Louis B. Mayer, Irene Mayer Selznick, and others in the fields with Hepburn.

He also remembers the chats his mom would have with Hepburn. The two became friends and, from time to time, Hepburn would give the family tickets to her stage performances and they were always invited back stage to chat after the shows. They would wait by a door and Hepburn's assistant, Phyllis Wilbourn, would come out and escort them to Hepburn.

Mark remembers one time the star gave them tickets to two of her shows, which turned out to be her last two plays. They went to the Shubert Theater in New Haven in 1975 to see *A Matter Of Gravity* and *The West Side Waltz* in Washington, D.C. Both times they had carte blanche to head back stage to talk to her.

The Bombaci family, like so many others Hepburn brought into her life, always protected her privacy. Mark said whenever Hepburn came to the farm, his mom would call to him to get a hold of his dad and tell him that Katharine Hepburn was coming down to pick and that he should put her by herself somewhere. Even so, Mark says

Circa early 1930s

her distinctive voice would carry and anybody out in the field at the time knew darn well who was among them gathering fruit. While he says people didn't bother her, he's pretty sure they gladly listened to her conversations with whomever she had brought along with her at the time!

"MY GREATEST STRENGTH IS...
COMMON SENSE. I'M REALLY
A STANDARD BRAND—LIKE
CAMPBELL'S TOMATO SOUP OR
BAKER'S CHOCOLATE."
—katharine hepburn

Mark remembers his mom telling him about Hepburn's discovery of the place. She said she stopped in front of the house and asked if this was a place to pick blueberries. Jo walked closer to the driver side window to answer the woman and knew right away who it was.

"Yes, Miss Hepburn, this is the place," she answered. Mark says his mom introduced herself to the star and told her how to get down to the field.

"Mother also had a flower garden, and she would allow Hepburn to pick as many flowers as she would like whenever she wanted," remembers Mark. They knew Hepburn loved flowers. Mark says she would take the flowers home and arrange them at her place in Fenwick and paint them. She liked to do watercolors of flowers.

According to Mark, Hepburn's choice of dress for the picking was just what you would expect. "She looked exactly the way you saw her in photographs," he said. "She wore pants and long sleeves; she was always fully covered because of her fair complexion. She would have a hat and scarf, just so very casual." He said she could be "feisty and strong-willed, but was always kind with a good sense of humor." He recalled one day she noticed a cat going after a bird under the blueberry netting and was going to have none of what was about to happen. According to Mark, Hepburn said, "Sorry, but I kicked one of your cats. She was nearing a bird and I didn't like that. I was just not going to allow it." He remarked they found it so funny, but caring, that she wasn't going to have a bird lose its life on her watch.

The Bombaci family's farm was unique in that it was situated along the Connecticut shoreline. They ran a small produce stand near the house with some fruits and vegetables for sale and then they added the blueberry fields. Mark told me Hepburn was of course in her advanced years when they came to know her, but she continued to come periodically during the summertime until about 1990 or so. They had a long and casual relationship with Hepburn for all those years. He told me even after his father died and the family ceased their pick-your-own berries operation, Hepburn would just drop by to say hi to Jo. Mark remembers she brought her mother flowers and her condolences following the death of his dad in the summer of 1988. He saw the two of them crying together over the loss. Mark says Hepburn was very considerate of others and certainly to his family.

Hepburn remembered their other family milestones as well. For his brother's wedding, she sent a "bottle" in celebration of the marriage. She brought them autographed photos of herself for the family, which they knew was special, as she did not often give out her signature to folks. Mark said the autographed photos of Hepburn still hang in his bedroom to this day. He also has ten or twelve notes that she had written to him and to his mother. One of the notes was a thank you to him after he sent her flowers while she was on stage in Washington, D.C. All of the notes were on Hepburn's official stationary with her name at the top in red, Katharine Houghton Hepburn. According to Mark, Hepburn would dictate to her secretary Phyllis Wilbourn what she would like the note to say. That part would be written on a typewriter, and then Kate herself would handwrite a note on it and sign it.

Mark says he used to joke with her about the lighthouse near her home in Fenwick. You can get to the lighthouse by just walking to it. He told her that he and his friends used to sneak out to it. She told him, "Oh you don't need to sneak out there, you go out there anytime you want. I give you permission." That meant he had the right to go onto her property to get to it—that was a big deal, as she hated when people trespassed on her property. It happened all of the time, once folks figured out where she lived they wanted to try and get a glimpse of her.

Bombaci also met Hepburn's only husband, Ludlow "Luddy" Ogden Smith when the two came by one day for berries. It was just the two of them that day, and Hepburn introduced him to the family.

In October 1973, Katharine Hepburn just showed up one day on the set of the *Dick Cavett Show* after Cavett had spent much time trying to get her first major television interview. It started when his producers asked her to do the show hoping they would have blind luck and she would say yes on the spot. She didn't. In fact, nothing happened. Cavett said when they didn't hear from her, he had all but given up on the idea.

But then Cavett attended a poolside party at Edward Albee's and, unbeknownst to him, started the ball rolling to get Hepburn on the set. Albee is a Pulitzer Prize–winning playwright who is best known for his 1962 *Who's Afraid of Virginia Woolf?*

"A woman took hold of my face and said, 'You don't know who I am, do you?'" said Cavett. "For whatever reason, I said, 'Betty Crocker?' She said, 'No, I'm Irene Mayer Selznick and I will encourage my friend Miss Hepburn to do your show.'"

Selznick was, of course, the daughter of the famed Louie B. Mayer, the American film producer and co-founder of Metro-Goldwin-Mayer Studios in Hollywood. Hepburn had told her friend Irene that she had been asked to do Cavett's show. He believes to this day that Irene turned the trick to get her on his show.

The Dick Cavett Show

That's when the "dance" with Cavett and Hepburn started. Cavett says it began with a fifteen-minute phone call. In the beginning of their conversation, according to him, she didn't say yes or no. As they talked further, she said, "Well, I'm inclined to do this, but if it goes badly, we'll just burn the tapes, won't we?"

To that statement he was thinking to himself, *Yeah right, we'll just throw all that money out the window and get rid of the interview.* Out loud he said, "Oh sure." Hepburn also insisted that prior to any possible interview, Cavett had to meet with Hepburn at her place in New York City so she could size him up.

He agreed. All of his groundwork netted a two-hour interview, the likes of which had never been seen before on television, and it was golden.

Hepburn decides to show up on the set, but not on the day she was scheduled; she was on Hepburn time. She waltzes in and catches everybody off guard. People started to scramble because they had her in the building, perhaps this was "go time."

Cavett said she was impulsive and wanted it her way. She said to the studio crew, "Well, why don't we do it now?" Nobody was ready for what started to unfold, they were all in shock that she was indeed going to sit down and do the show.

Cavett said that right away she started with her antics. Her attention to detail kicked in, and so did her boldness. Hepburn was a perfectionist.

"Nobody I ever had on the show had come in first to see the studio, to see where they would be sitting," said Cavett. "She wanted to see what the chair would be like, and what the rug would be like, and all those things." He chuckled just thinking back on what happened that day. He said that's when the light bulb went off in my head.

He motioned to have the cameras start rolling on everything she was doing, bossing people around, everything. All of her fussing about the set, he wanted it on tape in case that's all they got. All of her pregaming demands and people jumping to make things happen to make her happy is now a popular video on Youtube, it was pure Hepburn.

He recalls one his favorite moments during her rearrangement of the set. He says, "There was a piece of a fence on the set. She wanted to know who put it there and "couldn't we do without it?" A stagehand told her it would be a hassle to move, that they would have to take the whole thing apart. She replied, "Don't tell me what's wrong, just fix it."

Hepburn rearranged the whole set and continued to chastise the studio crew. On and on she went about the atrocious color of the carpeting, she wanted a stool to put her feet on, she wanted to see what she could reach, she kept looking around for things she could trouble people about, including wanting a box of tissue. She wanted to put people in their place, knock them out of their comfort levels for some reason.

All along they were never even sure if, after all her demands on the set, she would really sit for an interview. The guessing with her went on and on. But so far, Cavett knew he had the "visit to the studio" on tape. He thought at least they would have that to keep if she just walked out, but he didn't feel completely comfortable with what he was doing; he felt he was kind of cheating her, "sneaking one in on the great Kate."

She apparently was unaware of the cameras rolling, so he thought he should come clean and tell her that he had all of what she had been doing on tape. Her reply was, "Well, goodbye, Mr. Cavett, forever. I'll send someone in to see what you just got on tape."

He said he was thinking to himself, *Oh, thank God, we're still on the hook here. Maybe she'll be okay with what we got, I think we're still in the game.*

Cavett was told that a woman had come up to ABC to see the footage. He was thinking it was probably Hepburn's secretary. He asked what the woman looked like, and they told him they couldn't tell because "she had on a bush jacket and slacks and sandals and a scarf . . . and a babushka-like thing that covered most of her face." He said that's when he realized it was Hepburn herself who had shown up to see the tape. He still laughs about that.

Cavett says she never let on to him that she had seen the pre-interview fun and games with the crew. Cavett knew that was darn good television. He said it was one of the best ideas he had ever had in television, it was a marvelous piece of television history.

Hepburn told Cavett that she was told that the tape was "all right." He was so glad that he had gotten past the "sneaky little trick he had played on her."

Their interview, which Hepburn of course controlled, aired in two parts on television. This was a huge get for the legendary talk show host. Well-seasoned to many kinds of personalities, Cavett knew to just let it happen, to let Kate be Kate.

He told me Hepburn did not understand television at all. She never asked where the cameras would be, and during the interview he was never aware of her ever "playing" to a camera. He has watched the footage over and over again. She was a master of film, but this was a new medium for her. He thinks she was actually nervous on camera, being unsure about how television worked. But, as always, she threw herself into things that scared her to conquer them.

"If there were a snake in the room and everyone was afraid to deal with it," said Cavett. "I am certain she would pick it up and throw it out the window." Cavett says she was always challenging herself and that's why she finally did a television interview. It just happened to be with him. He could hardly get anyone to believe that she was indeed not comfortable on camera at first, mainly because she was Hepburn.

He says in the first minute or so her left cheek was twitching. You can't see it on tape, because that part of her face was away from the camera, but he noticed it right away. He says it was unmistakable, she was indeed nervous. She may have been clever enough to situate herself in such a manner on the set where the viewer would not notice that. Cavett says that knowing she was nervous relaxed him right away and gave him a kind of "upper hand." It wasn't long, though, before she got comfortable and began to have fun at his expense. She went to town on him, making fun of this or that. He knew there was no reason to stop it.

"A funny thing happened on that show," remembers Cavett. " I was desperate for things to say, and she made it easy so that my mind began to flow." But then he began to fear he wouldn't have enough time with her. As he got more and more into the interview, it occurred to him to talk about actor Laurence Olivier.

"You two have never acted together," he said.

"Well, neither of us is dead yet," Hepburn replied.

It turns out that someone watching the interview in Hollywood must have heard that the two had never worked together and ended up pairing Hepburn and Olivier in the 1975 made-for-television movie *Love Among The Ruins.*

The interview continued and Cavett said at one point she looked at him and told him she "was the most fascinating woman in the world."

"Nobody was like Hepburn," he said.

The day after the first of the two parts of her interview aired on television, Cavett chatted with Hepburn. She told him she was very happy about the show and she was getting reactions from "everywhere."

Hepburn was sixty-six years old when she did the Cavett interview. "You've made me a goddamned saint," she told him. "I walk down the street and people yell from windows, "We loved you last night.""

"She was quite startled at the reaction," Cavett chuckles. He says that Hepburn, the motion picture star, probably had no idea how many people watched his show or television in general.

Dick Cavett recalls the first time he laid eyes on Hepburn, decades before his interview with her. He was a junior at Yale University studying drama in 1957. This was Hepburn's first summer at the Shakespeare Festival Theater in Connecticut.

"It was the summer at Stratford," remembers Cavett. "I had just gotten there a couple days late from Nebraska where I grew up. We were all sitting in the theater getting notes from the director about staging and how the summer would go. All of a sudden, coming

The Philadelphia Story on Broadway (1939)

unannounced through the door was the great Katharine Hepburn. She walked down the aisle and everybody stopped what they were doing and just stared. I took full note of what was happening. She was in her everyday costume—sandals, slacks, and a jacket. She walked to the very front row and faced the group. You could feel a shock wave go through the room—awe, envy, just stunning star quality. I thought, *My God, this is the star of* African Queen, Summertime! All of her films began to go through my head."

By this time Hepburn had changed her position in the room slightly. Cavett is sure she had to feel the effect she was having on everybody in the room. He said you could "almost feel her star quality strike the surface of your skin as she passed by."

"That moment was just startling," he remembers. "She looked like a million bucks."

Cavett remembers that Hepburn chose to stay in the tiny red house on the theater's property while she worked there. It sat on the mouth of the Housatonic River and was just a bait shack on stilts, he recalls. He remembered her having many famous visitors there, including British playwright Noel Coward, actress Gene Tierney, and Spencer Tracy. She would venture out for a swim from it every day, even in rough waters. Someone remarked that the current might sweep her away, and someone else answered that it wouldn't dare. Nobody messed with Hepburn, not even Mother Nature.

Joan Kramer had a front row seat to Hollywood. She and her long-time British storytelling partner David Heeley documented the most famous people in entertainment from film and television. They worked together first at public television's WNET in New York City and then for their own production company, Top Hat Productions.

In Kramer's early days as an assistant talent coordinator for *The Dick Cavett Show,* she honed her skills for finding and booking guests. Even when those guests didn't want to be found or they resisted, she could wrangle them in. Kramer and Heeley were quite the duo, a crack team. They would go on to win numerous Emmys and other prestigious awards; their profiles were second to none. They were perfectionists, two parts of a well-oiled machine when it came to handling personas and egos.

> "HEPBURN WAS A FORCE OF NATURE. SHE WAS LIKE NOBODY ELSE I'D EVER MET. NO ONE CAME CLOSE TO THE LIKES OF HEPBURN. SHE WAS AN AMAZING LADY."
>
> —joan kramer

In 2015 they put all their tales into a book called *In The Company Of Legends.* It is chock-full of their times with screen and television legends, which included Katharine Hepburn. Kramer was the phone

The West Side Waltz on Broadway (1981)

person of the team, and she worked it like nobody's business. She learned that to land the bigger fish sometimes you had to call their friends and acquaintances first. Through persistence, hard work, and thoroughness, they landed them all. Kramer and Heeley were trusted confidantes and that, in the long run, made them successful. They told the stories of the biggest stars.

In 1980, they interviewed the legendary Katharine Hepburn in a show called *Starring Hepburn*. Many stars signed on to discuss their experiences working with the star, though Kramer believes they checked with Hepburn first before agreeing to do it. The film aired a year later and showcased Hepburn's career. At the time, Hepburn was on the road starring in what would be her last stage play *The West Side Waltz*. Kramer received a letter from Hepburn who said her family gave it rave reviews and that satisfied her. She told them she hadn't seen it, but that soon they would all get together and watch it. While that never happened, they were invited to tea with her. When they walked in the door Hepburn said to them, "So you're the two that did it."

"Guilty as charged," replied Kramer, and that was the beginning of an eighteen-year relationship that would net more documentaries with Hepburn.

Kramer believes that Hepburn had seen the show. Their spies told them she had let slip some things from the show she would not have known if she hadn't seen it, including saying that movie director George Cukor looked so young in it. The show ended up being nominated for an Emmy, to which Kate said to Kramer. "It deserves to be nominated for an Emmy, a goddamned good show should win."

A couple of months after the show aired, Kramer got a call from Hepburn.

"Hi, it's Kate Hepburn," she said. "Now that I have friends at public television, why don't we do another show together about Spencer?"

"That's when I almost fell on the floor," remembers Kramer. She said her mouth just dropped open at this news. She wasn't sure how she had the wherewithal to say, "Miss Hepburn, I'm getting another call. Would you mind if I put you on hold so I can tell them I will call them back?"

"Sure, go ahead," Hepburn replied.

She put Hepburn on hold and screamed for her partner Heeley. "Katharine Hepburn is on the phone asking us to do a show on Spencer Tracy!"

"Ask her if she'll host it," he replied.

Without time to think, Kramer got back on the line, saying, "Miss Hepburn, I'm back. Would you be willing to host the show on Spencer Tracy?

"Of course I'll host the show," the star replied loudly. "What do you think I'm talking about? Come to tea tomorrow." The dynamic duo of Kramer and Heeley had done it again!

Kramer believes she and Heeley really did come to know the real Hepburn beyond the star's façade over the years. She has chronicled this and so much more in their book. She maintains that Hepburn knew exactly what she was doing at all times, she knew what was right for her, Kramer says, even down to the red socks she wore under what Hepburn called her "rags." She was constantly in step with her persona.

In 1993 Kramer and Heeley did a show with Hepburn called *Katharine Hepburn: All About Me.* Hepburn was eight-five years old and said, "That creature I created needs a lot of attention in order to remain fascinating. Have I succeeded? Who knows?" She went on to say, "This is about Katharine Hepburn. Public or private, can you tell which is which? Sometimes I wonder myself."

Kramer believes her so-called "trans-Atlantic accent" was really how she talked, that it was not "put on." She says much of the family spoke the same way. She says Hepburn's sister Peg spoke the exact same way.

Kramer says Hepburn loved *All About Me,* and told her, "I don't know how much they paid you to do this, but it wasn't enough." Kramer admits that when they showed her the final product, it was terrifying.

Kramer says, no doubt about it, Hepburn was unique. There are no qualifiers to the word *unique.* Kramer says the actress was funny and astute at knowing that when she was self-deprecating, she was endearing.

> "IF FIRE WERE PUT UNDER MY NAILS I WOULD HAVE TO SAY SHE WAS THE MOST EXTRAORDINARY WOMAN I'D EVER MET."
> —david heeley

Over the years there were so many lunches, dinners, and teas with Hepburn that Kramer became a "repertoire" player for them as they continued with documentaries on other stars. She was interviewed on the shows they did about Jimmy Stewart, Humphrey Bogart, Henry Fonda, and many more.

Looking back on her time with Hepburn, Joan Kramer misses the lunches and teas and conversations they had. Kramer remembers being in the office one day and Hepburn called and told her she had been trying to reach her.

"I never get sick," she told Kramer, "but I have some kind of a stomach bug and I've been in bed for three days in Fenwick."

Kramer asked her if she was feeling better, admitting she wasn't feeling so great herself.

"You want a piece of advice?" the star asked her? "Go home and throw up, you'll feel a lot better."

Circa 1938

Katharine Hepburn became friends with Chester Erskine,
a Broadway director and producer during the 1930s who then went
on to write, produce, and direct Hollywood movies in the 1940s
and '50s. Erskine was also one of the first people in Hollywood to
recognize the acting ability of Spencer Tracy. In Tracy's early days, he
was thought by many to be "unphotographical." Erskine believed in
him and is known as the guy who gave Tracy his "big push forward."
Hepburn of course knew this and remembered it. When Erskine died
at the age of eighty-three, his wife Sally came to live with Hepburn.

Because television personalities Joan Kramer and David Heeley
were so entrenched in Hepburn's life, they, too, became friends with
Sally. One night the duo asked Sally to dinner and of course asked
Hepburn too.

"Where are you going?" Hepburn asked.

They told her they were taking Sally to Windows On The World,
the restaurant on the 107th floor of the North Tower of the World
Trade Center.

"That's very fancy," said Hepburn. "I'm not going to go to dinner,
but you can give me the money you would pay for my dinner." Kramer
chuckles when she thinks about that Hepburn reply.

Another time the two took Sally for a drive out to Kate's old
dear friend Laura Harding's home in New Jersey. Harding was a
very wealthy socialite, but was not doing well at the time. She lived
on a huge historic estate known as Bayonet Farm (so named because
Harding found a bayonet in the chimney of the main house) with
grounds that she would eventually give to the state of New Jersey.

Hepburn didn't join them for the adventure, but Kramer says she called them a million times to make sure they had the correct directions to Harding's home.

"You know it's very tricky to get there, you can get lost you have to take the right turn off the highway, when you get there call me," she said.

"She was like a mother hen," said Kramer. "She was very concerned."

When they arrived, Kramer told Harding that Kate had been toying around with coming out with them.

"Thank God she didn't come," said Harding. "Every time she comes she brings her own food, as if we have no food in this house!"

Harding was a multi-millionaire with housekeepers and cooks and a whole staff to run the estate. "Every time Kate comes, she brings steaks and potatoes and corn and insists that we have her food, and of course I always had food already prepared," she said.

Harding was in the first scene of Hepburn's 1932 movie *A Bill Of Divorcement*. You see her in the film coming down the stairs behind Hepburn, but her career did not take off and she gave up acting.

Joan Kramer remembers a story about Katharine Hepburn that she included in her book. She says it speaks volumes about who Katharine Hepburn was. A young intern attending Amherst College in Massachusetts was working as a production assistant on location at Hepburn's home in Fenwick. Somehow a raspberry had stained its way into a white chair in the room in which they were shooting. The intern discovered it when she was alone in the room and was worried that the crew would be blamed. Soon after, Hepburn walked into the room. The intern became so flustered that she ended up showing Hepburn. As Kramer put it, the young woman was terrified. Hepburn walked over to the chair, turned over the cushion, and told her there was now no longer a problem.

According to Katharine Hepburn's great niece Schuyler Grant, the woman was not a patient commuter. She never wanted to wait like ordinary people when driving on the highway. Enter what is known to the family as the "pig lane."

Hepburn often traveled to her place in New York, and was driven by her chauffer, Jimmy. When traffic got backed up on I-95 into the city, she would shout, "Pig lane!" That meant she wanted Jimmy to drive in the brake-down lane to get around the bumper-to-bumper traffic and get her where she needed to go. This practice was always to the horror of her driver, but Grant says Hepburn did it often and, accordingly, was often stopped by police. As you might imagine, when

Circa 1940

they did get pulled over, the officer would look in the back seat and see that it was the great Katharine Hepburn and would always give the star a pass, telling her and her driver to never to do it again. She never listened.

Katharine Hepburn was fascinated by Michael Jackson. According to her great niece Schuyler Grant, it wasn't so much that she cared about his music, but that she admired his incredible talent and related to his worldwide fame. Hepburn went to some of his concerts at Madison Square Garden and invited him to her New York townhouse. On one or two occasions Grant, as a teenager, was there too for dinner with the King of Pop and others. Grant says he was just socially odd. He was quiet and introverted yet would occasionally burst out with a story, such as the one about how, as a child, he and his siblings would watch their pet snake eat live mice, hardly dinnertime talk. But Hepburn, a great conservationist, would keep things moving in uncomfortable moments like this and steer the conversation away from mice and snakes. Grant said that her aunt wanted to know how he came to be so famous, and she spent a lot of time with him to figure that out.

May 12, 2010, was an important day at the Katharine Hepburn Cultural Arts Center in Katharine Hepburn's beloved hometown of Old Saybrook, Connecticut. Not only would it have been Hepburn's 103rd birthday, but it was also the day that her beautiful US postage stamp was to be unveiled. Actor Sam Waterston, who co-starred with Hepburn in the 1973 television film *The Glass Menagerie*, was master of ceremonies. Waterston unveiled the stamp alongside US Postmaster General John (Jack) E. Potter. British filmmaker Anthony Harvey was also on stage. Harvey had directed Hepburn in the 1968 film *The Lion in Winter*, for which he earned an Academy Award nomination and Hepburn received her third Oscar.

Designed by Derry Noyes, art director for the US Postal Service, Hepburn's 44-cent, first-class stamp is based on a 1942 publicity shot by photographer Clarence S. Bull from Hepburn's film *Woman of the Year*. It was part of a series of stamps dedicated to the "Legends of Hollywood." Noyes completely captures the beauty and thespian brilliance Hepburn personified.

> "WHAT YOU SEE BEFORE YOU,
> MY FRIEND IS THE RESULT OF A
> LIFETIME OF EATING CHOCOLATE!"
> —katharine hepburn

Katharine Hepburn loved chocolate. One of her favorite places to get her sweets from was Mondel Chocolates in New York City, which opened in 1943 and still exists today. She loved the chocolate pecan turtles and, according to the shop as reported by *The New York Times* in 2015, other favorites were molasses chips, butter crunch, dark orange peel, champagne truffles, and dark almond bark. Customers still come in and ask for the "Hepburn mix."

Hepburn's grand nice Schuyler Grant claims her aunt would go through about a pound of chocolate a week, but somehow always kept her very slight figure. When she turned ninety in 1997, Mondel Chocolates sent her chocolates.

Katharine Hepburn has fans around the world, including Dr. Natalia Konik, an eye surgeon from Paris, France. Dr. Konik is an ophthalmologist who practices at L'Hospital Charles Foix-Jean Rostaud of the Assistance Publique Hopitaux. She is such a huge Hepburn fan that she purchased one of the red theater chairs that

A Bill of Divorcement (1932) with David Manners

went into The Kate. These were being sold to raise money for the venue, and she wanted to have a stake as a founder even though she was a world away.

In her home across the world, she has many photos of Katharine Hepburn, and some signed letters too. She has every single book that has been written about the star and all her movies. She shows the movies in a home cinema in her Paris flat. She has so much memorabilia that she has a complete Kate room in honor of Hepburn.

Holiday (1938) with Cary Grant

epilogue

Ellsworth Grant recalled: After making *On Golden Pond* and recovering from her December 1982 automobile accident, Katharine's popularity was never greater said her brother-in-law Ellsworth Grant. The two books she wrote, *The Making of the African Queen* and *Me,* won her a host of new fans. She spent several hours every day personally responding to the hundreds of letters pouring in. But fame and wealth were not enough; she couldn't enjoy them. Her nervous energy compelled her to move back and forth from New York to Fenwick. Her qualities of independence, tenacity, and non-stop working did not give her peace of mind.

When she was writing her book *Me,* she sometimes read me a chapter, and once we fell to discussing why "A-type" men and women strive so hard and so long and after succeeding feel restless and unhappy. I suggested it was the pursuit not the achievement that was exciting and compelling, an idea she found fascinating.

She realized she had run out of pursuits; she had done it all, there was nothing more to win.

> "IF YOU WANT TO CHANGE ATTITUDES, START WITH A CHANGE IN BEHAVIOR."
>
> —katharine hepburn

Nevertheless, she clung tenaciously to life. After a bout of pneumonia at the age of eight-nine, Katharine abandoned her New York brownstone and settled in Fenwick. Of course she could no longer play tennis or golf, but she could, and did, swim daily. She had no interest in religion, like her father and mother, but she admired Dr. James Kidd, the pastor of the Asylum Hill Congregational Church in Hartford. He had conducted the memorial service for Marion in 1986. She chided him on his reading of the 23rd Psalm and invited him to come to Fenwick where she would tape for him the way she felt the emotion in the word should be conveyed.

In 1996, she continued to decline. The family thought another visit by Dr. Kidd might console her. Her spirits revived and she told the doctor, "I'm not ready to die yet."

The end of her remarkable journey came on June 29, 2003 at her seaside home in Fenwick.

Joan Kramer remembers her final goodbye to Katharine Hepburn. She and Heeley had gone to visit Hepburn's brother-in-law Ellsworth Grant and his second wife, Virginia (Hepburn's sister Marion had died years prior, and Grant had remarried), who lived down the way from Kate in Fenwick.

After lunch with Ellsworth and Virginia, Kramer and Heeley went down the road to Kate's place. Kate was sitting on a couch in the living room and they had one of their usual spirited discussions, as well as some of her delicious brownies with mocha chip ice cream, which was her favorite. Kramer says Hepburn was "a little fuzzy" and having trouble remembering whether some of the people she had worked with over the years were still living.

"There was a different mode of conversation," remembers Kramer. "It was not the normal, full-of-beans Kate." When she and Heeley left that day from Fenwick, Heeley said, "I don't want to see her again." He wanted to remember the vibrant Kate, not the one who was starting to fail. They had known the real Kate, and that's how he wanted to remember her forever.

Kramer and Heeley found Hepburn very easy to love. They found her "smart, very, very smart; very funny; and very astute. She got somebody's number very quickly. She caught on to who people were all about," said Kramer.

"Hepburn believed in paddling her own kayak, which allowed her to be in control at all times," said Kramer. "As a woman, she was an influence that was profound. You can't be around her and not be awed at what she accomplished in her lifetime. It was a privilege to work with Hepburn all those years and to be her friend."

Hepburn was free to be herself in Old Saybrook everyone respected her privacy. She could be free from the spotlight and even more so in the tight-knit borough of Fenwick. From time to time she would get groceries at Walt's Food Market in town, but nobody bothered her, she was just Kate.

Toward the end of her life, Gene Heiney, childhood friend to Hepburn's nephew, Tor, and Old Saybrook police detective, remembers helping her get tucked into bed in her room on the second floor of her house overlooking the water.

"She held my hand and her eyes were as clear as a bell. She knew her time left on Earth was short. I leaned over her and gave her a kiss. That was the last time I saw her."

A few weeks later she passed. Gene was off duty, but sprang into action for Kate. It was time to put his well-laid-out plan for privacy into play, keep the press at bay, and give this icon her due. It was time to let her go out the way she wanted.

Once word began leaking that the great Katharine Hepburn was gone, media from around the world tried to descend upon Fenwick. Little did all of us know that Gene was firing on all cylinders to protect Miss Hepburn. He would turn out to be a formidable opponent for the press.

Circa 1929

Gene was in "go mode." He got the call, was sad, but went to work as a police officer with a plan to protect Hepburn, her family, and Fenwick from the glare of the media. As it turned out, Hepburn was long gone before the press got to town. Gene said he had known that there may be boats and helicopters ready for this moment in history to get all kinds of photos and video. He knew they would sit outside her beach and that choppers would hover in the air.

He took care of the boat issue, as he was in charge of the marine patrol in Old Saybrook. He had the police boat come out and sit in front of her house. He also had called the captain of the port in New Haven and told him he was closing a section of Long Island sound around Old Saybrook.

"I was not going to allow any boat within a certain distance of her house," Gene said.

The captain told him he could not do that, and he said, "I'm doing it anyway. That's how personal I took her death and my promise to protect her memory and her property. I had known her since I was four years old."

He remembers that one of the large media networks somehow got a news truck into Fenwick. It came roaring across the nine-hole golf course to get to her house, which sent Fenwick residents into a tailspin. That truck was banished from the area as quickly as it had gotten in.

The air space over Fenwick was set to be closed, too. As it turned out, that plan didn't have to be implemented because there was such a thick marine fog on the day Hepburn died. Aircraft just wouldn't be able to go up.

There were two Old Saybrook police cars at the front entrance of Fenwick and the press was staged outside of her community. Gene said he only took one network pool reporter inside Fenwick to get a couple of shots of her home and that was it.

Gene says he misses Hepburn to this day, more than a decade later. "That old New England–style gal was a real person, there was nothing phony about her, nothing phony at all. She was a person who lived in an age that doesn't exist anymore."

When Hepburn died in the summer of 2003, everyone in Fenwick worried about what would become of her home. Who would be its new caretaker? So many in the borough had spent time there at one time of their lives that they all felt a kind of endearing ownership and wanted it to go to the right family who understood its significance to the borough.

At the time of her death, the home had fallen into complete disrepair. Things had become too expensive to maintain . . . but the memories and its place in history was important.

As it turned out, the Hepburn home fell into very capable hands. Frank Sciame, a prominent New York Builder and former chair of the New York Landmarks Conservancy, understands the history of buildings. He understands what architecture means in time and place.

He and his family had a cottage in Fenwick for about ten years prior to becoming the owners of the Hepburn Estate, the jewel of the borough. He bought the 3.4-acre estate in 2004, shortly after Hepburn's death.

The property came with 600 feet of beach on Long Island Sound at the mouth of the Connecticut River, with a breakwater and a pond in the expansive backyard near the famed Fenwick nine-hole golf course where Hepburn often played.

"It doesn't get any better than this," said Sciame. "The property was the king of the hill, it was Katharine Hepburn's, it's the only completely brick house in the borough, the whole package was intriguing including its pedigree."

Even though the Hepburns rebuilt the home using brick after the first all-wooden home had washed out to sea in the Hurricane of 1938, it eventually fell into disrepair as the years wore on. Sciame said when he took a look at the property, the bones were good but it truly was the quintessential handyman special. He believed that not much had been done to the house after it had been rebuilt in 1939 and that it would need a ton of work to really make it the home it should be in modern times. He said the house had settled a bit, was taking on water, and was listing, leaning, about 6 inches from the back of the house to the front. Sciame said when you walked in the house you felt the floors out of level. He found that to be pretty "extraordinary."

There is a bedroom above the garage in the home where you can see the leaning. Sciame also says if you look very closely at the fireplace, you can tell that the brick is not quite straight, it slopes down to the right above the fireplace screen. He says this is a tell-tale look at the home's history.

An enormous amount of updating and money was needed to make the grand home the way it should be. Sciame said after the building inspection, which he did himself, he offered the executors of the estate $6 million; it had initially been listed for $12 million. He gave the estate forty-eight hours to decide on his offer and said, "Honestly, half of me was hoping they would say yes, and the other half was hoping they said no." The answer was "yes."

The Sciames then became the new owners of a huge part of Hollywood and Connecticut history. They went to work quickly on the home to make it the best it could be in a modern world, but at the same time preserve its heritage. Sciame said his thoughts then turned to how was he going to maintain the exterior of the house and the character of the interior in terms of the fireplaces and the basic structure. He had to make it suitable for twenty-first-century living. Right off the bat, he said he realized he had to raise the home by 5 feet to protect it from the water. Because he had previous experience in his career as a builder with moving buildings, he knew he could do it.

Sciame gathered engineers and contractors from New York City to get the job done. He brought on friend and architect James D'Auria and the two of them did the layout of the interior of the house. Sciame's wife Barbara then did the interior decorating. All this happened very quickly. They bought the property in September 2004 and wanted to be in the home for their yearly August vacation in Fenwick in 2005;

they got it done. Sciame says even he can't believe they met their goal.

His builder, Rich Finnegan from Old Saybrook, Connecticut, told him it was the worst experience and best experience of his career.

When the Sciames retained ownership of the house, most of the contents were gone except for a few photos and etchings and an audio cassette recording of the first television interview Hepburn did on *The Dick Cavett Show* in the 1970s. There were teapots and a few dishes around, too, said Sciame. He said right after they bought the house and before the renovations started, he began getting emails from Hepburn fans. He said one woman wrote saying her husband asked her what she wanted for her birthday and she said all she wanted was to see the inside of the Katharine Hepburn house. Sciame, saying he is an old softie, invited her to the house. She came and saw an old teapot. She asked if it was Hepburn's (it was), and he just gave it to her. He invited others into the house, too, who had written to him. He marveled at the enormous amount of fans who still loved her.

Also left behind were the kerosene cooking range, and a refrigerator. I saw that vintage "icebox" when I toured the home with builder, Rich Finnegan. It is tucked away in the garage behind one of the golf carts that is the mode of transportation around Fenwick in the summertime. It is a beauty!

Sciame said the kitchen was in terrible shape. The refrigerator was up on cement blocks, perhaps because of the water that would occasionally come into the house. There are stories that the Hepburn family had pegs on the wall on which they would place the chairs when water came in. After things dried up, down the chairs would go again. It is amazing that Hepburn had entertained the biggest stars in Hollywood right there in that old kitchen.

Sciame, ever the builder, maintains that the Hepburns could have stopped the water over the years if they had just put a berm at the pond in the back of the house. He said, "It was so unfortunate that they didn't do that because it would not have been that expensive. They just didn't realize that the water wasn't coming from the Sound, it was coming from the pond in the back of the house." He and Finnegan figured out that the pond was the problem when the garage, which they did not raise in the renovation, was getting flooded.

Sciame preserved the portion of the concrete sea wall at the house that has all the Hepburn and Houghton names carved into it, including Katharine's. This has a special meaning to his family and for anyone who visits the house.

Sciame explained what it is like to be the owner, the caretaker, of Katharine Hepburn's home, the place in which the legendary screen actress spent much of her life.

"I like history, he said. "I like old buildings. I am past chairman of the Landmarks Conservancy in New York City, at which I was leading an organization where we were the stewards of all the great buildings in Manhattan—Grand Central Station, the Farley Post Office Building, all of these great buildings. Being a good steward is engrained in me, and I look at the Hepburn house as something special. It was the place where a very, very great family lived. Katharine Hepburn was the most famous, but her father was a great doctor and her mother was at the forefront of women's suffrage movement. This family had such great respect for each other. I think it's important to be the steward of that place."

When the house was finished in August 2005, Sciame and his family were about to sit down for lunch when two people showed up. An elderly man came walking in with a walker accompanied by an older woman. They were Hepburn's brother, Bob, and sister, Peg. They had come to tour their old home. Sciame asked them if they wanted to join the family for lunch. They all ate together and then they toured the home. Sciame said as they made their way through the house, the two Hepburn siblings would say, "Dad would have loved this," and "Dad would have done that." Sciame found this unannounced experience amazing. That the remaining Hepburns were at peace with what he had done to the place meant the world to him. This was, after all, the place in which the Hepburn children had spent their summers. They grew up in the house. They told him they loved how the house had taken shape. Sciame said, "It made me feel so good, what they said."

Peg died less than a year later in February 2006 at the age of eighty-five. Bob passed away in November 2007 at the age of ninety-four.

Sciame sums up the place in which he has found a new home this way: "Fenwick is an absolute unique community. You wake up on a Saturday morning and find bicycles that have been left all over the place. It's like one big, private playground. The kids get to know each other, the parents get to know each other, there are these unwritten rules. The parents and the kids can be together, but as the sun goes down in the summer the kids disperse and the parents then enjoy a cocktail or two together. There are all kinds of events planned in the homes of people who summer there. If one couple has a party, it's pretty much known that you open the doors for anyone in the borough who wants to show up. For the kids there are sailing and swimming camps, tennis, and golf, all there right on the grounds of Fenwick." There is a golf tournament every year called The Morgan Cup. If you win, you have to host a party for the whole community. Everybody brings food, but you're on the hook for the place. He says he understands why, since the 1890s, the place is so loved. There are not many places like it in the world.

Per Katharine Hepburn's will, there was to be no memorial service or funeral for her. She requested that her ashes be interred in the family plot at Cedar Hill Cemetery in Hartford, Connecticut.

about the author

Ann Nyberg is the longest-serving, full-time anchor/reporter in Connecticut television history, anchoring the news at WTNH-TV (ABC) in New Haven. She began her broadcast journalism career right after graduation from Purdue University with a degree in journalism. Highlights of her career include assignments to Cuba and to the Vatican. She also hosts her own on-air and online long format chat show called *Nyberg,* on which she interviews innovators, entrepreneurs, and everyday folk, anybody who has a story to tell. Her popular website, "Network Connecticut," spotlights people, places, innovators, entrepreneurs, and small businesses all over the state. She has been nominated for multiple Emmys and, in November 2015, was inducted into the prestigious Silver Circle. This is an honor given to television professionals who have made significant contributions to their communities and to the vitality of the television industry. It is a special recognition given to television pioneers by the

National Academy of Television Arts & Sciences (NATAS) Boston/ New England Chapter.

Ann has made significant contributions to her southern New England community, she is a founding Board of Trustees member of the Katharine Hepburn Cultural Arts Center (The Kate) in Old Saybrook, Connecticut, and is the only honorary female member of the Walter Camp Football Foundation, which raises thousands of dollars every year for charity. In 1993, Ann founded the Toy Closet Program at Yale-New Haven Hospital. Thousands of toys and other items are given to children of all ages to help ease their trauma.

Ann is the author of *Slices of Life, A Storyteller's Diary* (Homebound Publications, 2015) and also owns a boutique in Madison, Connecticut, called "Annie Mame," where she sells vintage items and things made in Connecticut.